SUCCESS
MUZZLELOADER
HUNTING

Pete Schoonmaker

©2004 by Peter Schoonmaker
Published by

kp books
An imprint of F+W Publications, Inc.

700 East State Street • Iola, WI 54990-0001
715-445-2214 • 888-457-2873

Our toll-free number to place an order or obtain
a free catalog is (800) 258-0929.

Library of Congress Catalog Number: 2004092784

ISBN: 0-87349-746-5

Designed by Paul Birling

Edited by Dan Shideler

Printed in United States of America

Dedication

Robert J. Schoonmaker Jr.

During the last 25 years my father has taken a great interest in my muzzleloading projects. Dad didn't shoot his first muzzleloading deer until 1981. Since bird dogs and upland game have always been his primary interest, he quickly adapted to the muzzleloader shotgun for partridge, woodcock, pheasants and wild turkeys.

My father enjoys shooting muzzleloader-hunting guns, ranging from traditionally-styled flintlock smoothbores at one end of the spectrum to the latest drop-action innovation in modern in-line rifles. From range testing to field performance, he will shoot and shoot and shoot until he discovers what a gun will do on paper at the shooting range and on game in the field.

For this outdoor writer who is responsible for several dozen articles a year, Dear Old Dad provides an immeasurable service. Although I often accompany him to the shooting range, he always perseveres to discover which projectile, shot load, and granulation of powder or pellet charge works the "best" in each muzzleloader tested. His habitual thoroughness has earned him the nickname R&D–short for "research and development."

This past autumn my 83-year old father once again took to the fields, deer hunted 27 days, and bagged a nice muzzleloading buck in the process. I never have to wonder if my father is ready to go hunting or shooting. I consider myself a very lucky son, and I am eternally grateful for the guidance, joy and knowledge he has provided about hunting, shooting, business and life.

Thanks, Dad!

About the Author

Pete Schoonmaker has been an outdoor writer for more than 20 years. He is well known for his in-the-field articles and photography that emphasize the enjoyment, challenge, and appreciation of hunting with primitive arms. Pete has written two other books in addition to *Successful Muzzleloader Hunting* and nearly 500 feature articles. He is a field editor for the International Blackpowder Hunting Association publication *Blackpowder Hunting* and *Whitetails Unlimited* magazine. As a feature writer, Schoonmaker is a frequent contributor to the National Muzzle Loading Rifle Association's publication *Muzzle Blasts*, Dixie Gun Works' *Blackpowder Annual*, *Buckmasters* and *Bow & Arrow Hunting*.

Acknowledgments

A book project is conceived, compiled and written by the author. But behind the scenes there are many inspirations and people that help make the book a reality. Although the actual physical writing of the text is not what you would call a social event, there are many special people, scenic places and remarkable things that make the book-writing experience a memorable one.

Since outdoor writing, hunting, travel and photography do not fall within the realm of the normal 8 to 5 working hours, a strong support system at home is essential. My wife of 26 years, Christine Ava, didn't even bat an eye when I crawled out at minus 28 degrees last weekend to go set a photo blind for bald eagles on a frozen river with fellow photographer Warren Greene. Chris often refers to her "favorite" quote of mine: "If I could just go on this caribou hunt with my father." Well, that was in 1981 and the rest, as they say, is history. I am forever grateful to Chris for her love and support. (For some reason she still isn't fond of my cleaning muzzleloaders in the house.)

In 1974, Lyman published its *Blackpowder Handbook.* It was the only book of its kind for the muzzleloading enthusiast. In 1985, a book titled *Sam Fadala's Muzzleloading Notebook* was published. It was the first and best book of its kind in the new era of muzzleloading.

Sam Fadala has been my greatest inspiration as a muzzleloading writer. His *Blackpowder Loading Manual* and *Blackpowder Handbook* are standards in the industry. No one in the modern era has burned more powder or tested more muzzleloading firearms, and compiled more technical data on the subject, than Sam Fadala. Sam reviewed, advised me on, and wrote the forward to my first book in 1992 and sponsored me into the Outdoor Writers Association of America. Sam recently rewrote Lyman's *Blackpowder Handbook & Loading Manual.* For several years in the late '80s and early '90s, Sam and I wrote the muzzleloading articles for *Trapper & Predator Caller.* Naturally, he wrote the technical pieces, while I did the hunting articles. We both are currently field editors for *Blackpowder Hunting* magazine.

My father joins many lucky men of his generation who survived WWII. In his case, it was 38 months in the Philippines and New Guinea in B-25s with the Army Air Corp bomber group known as the Air Apaches. A mission that went badly on November 6,1944 resulted in a late night ditching and survival for 7 days in the South China Sea. A self-employed carpenter, he remains semi-retired today, and celebrated 58 years of marriage with my mother Margie. A family-oriented man, he has always had his priorities: my mother, my brother Mark, our hunting dogs, and ME. We learned early that time isn't counted in years, but in decades of dogs. It was a totally entertaining learning experience growing up over the years with rabbit chasing beagle legends named Lula Bell, Sis, Sal and Duke; bird dogs that included regal and talented English setter pointers named Jake and Kate; a goofy Brittany named Suzie; and a happy-go-lucky springer spaniel named Sam.

I literally grew up hunting, following my grandfather Schoonmaker, my father and our dogs. It was bird hunting until the snow flew, cottontail rabbits until the snow got deep, and then it was snowshoe rabbits on snowshoes. I didn't play high school sports my senior year (I was mediocre at best) but I could bird hunt with my springer spaniel Sam and with my father and his woodcock and partridge pointing machine, an English setter named Jake. As Robert Ruark stated in the author's note to his masterpiece, *The Old Man and the Boy,* "Anybody who reads this book is bound to realize that I had a real fine time as a kid." And I did, too!

The following people have been very helpful over the years: Editor Maxine Moss published my very first article in the NMLRA publication *Muzzle Blasts* in 1982. Her successor, Sharon Cunningham, was the first editor to offer constructive criticism on my misuse of "dangling participles." Then again, I didn't even know that was a subject we could discuss! The current *Muzzle Blasts* editor, Terri Trowbridge, and Joyce Vogel, who heads up the Longhunter Muzzleloading Big Game Records, have been very helpful. Debra Bradbury of *Blackpowder Hunting* has been very supportive as an editor and very helpful with this book. Denise Dubick and Jeff Davis at *Whitetails Unlimited* magazine have been wonderful in their presentation of my muzzleloading material in their publication. Butch Winter, editor of the *Dixie Guns Works Blackpowder Annual* is due thanks for his long-standing interest in my hunting material, as are Sherry Kerr for keeping me up-to-date and informed with her Outdoor Media Resources, and Kevin Michalowski, firearms editor in the Books Division at KP Books, for presenting me with the idea of this book and making it happen.

The following cast of characters has in some way made this book possible: Art Green, Bob Avery, David Oathout, Don Robbins, Mark Putnam, Kurt Edwards, Clay Earley, Charlie Alsheimer, Larry Weishuhn, Tony Knight, Chris Hodgdon, L.D. Wayne, Gary Stoller, Billy Witts, Dr. Andy Baker, Joe Barone, Dick & Joyce Ploss, Warren Greene, Mike Jardine, Will Peabody, and the Rice Pond Gang: John Ward, Mark Schoonmaker, Mike Shafer, Steve Santa-Maria and Jay Ritter. To all of them I tender my very sincere thanks.

Contents

Introduction

There has never been a better time in history to be interested in muzzleloading guns than right now. The variety of quality guns and muzzleloader hunting opportunities has never been better. From a full-stock flintlock to a scoped stainless in-line in a synthetic stock, the choice is yours. Due to this broad spectrum of choices, we enter a new century with more people shooting muzzleloaders than ever before.

Obviously, I enjoy shooting and hunting with a wide variety of muzzleloaders. Some guns enhance my skills with high technology while others refresh my skills by requiring high technique. As you read *Successful Muzzleloader Hunting,* you will discover, as I have, that muzzleloader hunting is as diverse in the types of guns to hunt with as there is game to hunt.

A few years ago, a hunting publication displayed a photo of me with a fine whitetail buck shot during a regular firearms season with a modern in-line muzzleloader. A few weeks later I received a letter from a disgruntled reader who referred to my gun as "stainless steel and Tupperware" and to me as an "opportunity seeker who has no appreciation of the long rifle." The irony of the letter was that the very day that it arrived in the mail I had been with my father and springer spaniel Sadie hunting pheasants with a 20-gauge flintlock fowler. This beautiful full-stock smoothbore is my father's favorite fun-gun. When not in use it resides in a gun rack alongside in-lines, cap locks and side hammers, with single-barrel and double-barrel shotguns and rifles featuring curly maple, walnut, laminated, and synthetic stocks. And believe it or not, they all get along together just fine.

Muzzleloader hunting is a state of mind. *Successful muzzleloader loader hunting* is a state of satisfaction: satisfaction achieved by applying acquired shooting and hunting skills to the knowledge of habitat and the traits of the game hunted. Mountains, plains, farm country, forests and tundra are the hunting grounds available to muzzleloader hunters. Hunting favorite game on favorite hunting grounds is an annual ritual that completes the life of many muzzleloading hunters. Theodore Roosevelt stated it best: "In hunting, the finding and killing of the game is after all but a part of the whole. The free, self-reliant, adventurous life, with its rugged and stalwart democracy, the wild surroundings, the grand beauty of the scenery, the chance to study the ways and habits of the woodland creatures–all these unite to give to the career of the wilderness hunter its peculiar charm."

The National Muzzle Loading Rifle Association was formed in 1933. The NMLRA and its monthly publication *Muzzle Blasts* continue to promote our nation's rich historical muzzleloading heritage through educational and cultural venues such as match competition, hunting, safety, gun making and historical re-enactments. The International Blackpowder Hunting Association and its quarterly publication *Blackpowder Hunting* promote all forms of blackpowder shooting and contemporary muzzleloader hunting.

Muzzleloader hunting is alive and well today. I bought my first muzzleloading rifle on March 16, 1976. Through trial and error, muzzleloader hunting has taught me to be a better hunter while putting the hunt back into the hunting.

Pete Schoonmaker
March 2004

1

The Elements Of Successful Muzzleloader Hunting

When you first start muzzleloading, you'll experience that magical moment when you grasp a certain front-stuffer and are instantly fascinated with everything about it. How it feels in your hands, how its lock and trigger function, how it will shoot when you shoulder the rifle–all of this captures your imagination. It doesn't take long before you become familiar with the essentials of muzzleloading: ignition, propellant, and projectile. As your interest in muzzleloading swells, you might begin to wonder how our predecessors did as well as they did with these primitive shooting irons.

My muzzleloading career started with a crescent-butted, 45-caliber Thompson/Center Seneca half-stock rifle and a suede-fringed, over-the-shoulder shooting bag. My first trip to the shooting range in 1976 included a pound of FFg blackpowder, a package of patches, a box of round balls, a short starter, and a tin of percussion caps.

Like most things in life, experience was the best teacher. I aggressively hunted with that rifle for my first few introductory years of muzzleloading. It was during that period of exposure to primitive arms hunting that I discovered efficiency afield through inefficiency afield. Experience came painfully and involved things such as getting a patch accidentally folded over and a round ball stuck in the barrel with no way to remove it. This happened, of course, immediately after tracking down a 6-point buck on a dusting of snow and missing him, only to have the buck stand there and watch the cloud of smoke rise as I frantically attempted to reload. Lesson: a "good" ramrod has a built in ball puller.

Then there was the time in 1982 when I dropped my last lead ball onto the gravel floor of the tundra after making a solid hit on a bull caribou. Although a second shot was not needed, try finding a 45-caliber round ball in a sea of 45-caliber gravel. Speed loaders today carrying powder and projectile in one unit have since solved that particular problem. I've also had my share of range estimation problems in the big country, the high plains, and the Rocky Mountains. I have over-estimated, shooting just the over the back of a 15-inch buck pronghorn in Wyoming, and under-estimated, shooting just under a nice 5x5 bull elk in Colorado. Ah, yes.

THE BIG GAME WE HUNT

To me, game habitats are the most interesting part of hunting game with America's original shooting. Whitetail deer started my muzzleloader hunting interest in the Adirondacks, where I live and hunt today. From high peaks to foothills to the historic St. Lawrence, Champlain and Mohawk valleys, whitetails, black bear, wild turkeys, upland game and waterfowl can be found in the various habitats ranging from old timber "forever wild" forests to transition lands of mixed forest and agriculture, to fertile valleys with creek bottoms and alder beds. My first big game trip was to the tundra of northern Quebec in the early 1980s. What a contrast in terrain, with its lichen-covered boulders, scrub spruce, endless waterways and landscape with the amazing caribou carrying more antler than all the whitetails I had ever seen.

Wyoming's wide-open sagebrush country and cottonwood river bottoms on the high plains seemed like Africa with their unique pronghorn antelope herds and high-antlered mule deer. High, mountain Golden aspen meadows, ringing with the bugling of the bull elk of the Rocky Mountain autumn, should be experienced at least once by every muzzleloader hunter. And let's not forget

Without a doubt, the whitetail deer is the number one muzzleloader big game.

Knowing the traits, habits, and habitat of your intended game is the key to successful muzzleloader hunting.

Small game is where the action is, and the wild turkey is the big game of small game hunting.

the majestic moose that dwells from Alaska's plains, down the Rockies to Wyoming, the Canadian woodlands, and to Maine's dense forests.

The most popular muzzleloading big game animal in North America are whitetail deer. They are abundant and they are accessible to muzzleloader hunters from all walks of life. Hands down, whitetails are the number one muzzleloader hunting game species and the primary drive behind the muzzleloading firearms industry. The black bear, another blackpowder favorite, is also abundant from coast to coast. The romance of a high-country packhorse trip during the special muzzleloader-only September bugling season in the Rockies makes elk hunting a favorite for resident hunters and guided non-resident hunters alike. The Rocky Mountain states offer special mule deer seasons. But like other popular big game–pronghorn, moose, and caribou–the mule deer is often hunted during regular firearms season by hunters preferring to use the muzzleloader.

SMALL GAME /BIG ACTION

The big game of small game is the wild turkey. The spring event called turkey hunting has put the muzzleloading shotgun back on the map. With so many hunters looking between the hammers of a double-barrel, or lining up the fiber optics sights on a single barrel, turkey shotguns are a market unto themselves. Shotgunning for small game is an often-overlooked, action-packed muzzleloader event. From edge covers holding woodcock and grouse, to farm country pheasants and autumn turkeys, to briar patch cottontails and winter woodland white rabbits, shotgun hunting presents a lot of opportunities. Small game hunting with small caliber muzzleloaders is another fun outing waiting to be experienced. Varmints present yet another muzzleloader challenge. Groundhogs help rifle shooters become marksmen.

Muzzleloader hunters have one common goal: when the smoke clears, they want to see that their shot was true.

FUN HUNTING

When scouting for game, knowing the game animal's habits and routines and using the terrain to your advantage are essential. Still-hunting, glassing and stalking, and tracking are great ways to hunt big game under the right weather conditions. A well-scouted, well-placed treestand will be effective on a variety of big game, the most popular treestand-hunted game being the whitetail. Organized drives also work well to get game moving. But of all the hunting tactics, calling and decoying game into range can provide the muzzleloader with some of the most memorable hunting experiences. From barking gray squirrels to the enticing cow call of moose, from grunting whitetails to honking waterfowl, from gobbling turkeys to bugling elk, calling game to the muzzleloader is fun, exciting, and traditional, and it goes hand in hand with this primitive style of hunting.

The majority of adult muzzleloader hunters today started their hunting careers with grandpa's .22 rifle or 20-gauge shotgun in pursuit of small game. They may have started deer hunting with their father or uncle with a bolt-action rifle in the 30-caliber family. But something about hunting with America's original front-loading hunting gun appealed to them. Maybe it was the extended whitetail season, or a muzzleloader-only elk hunt. Or just maybe it is the romance and challenge of hunting with a blackpowder hunting gun. While some hunters are consumed by getting that 170 class buck, the majority of hunters are just pleased to fill their tag and put meat in the freezer on a day off from work in the deer woods. To be a successful muzzleloader hunter you have to put yourself in the position to get a shot at the game of your intent. But first, you have to know and understand these guns we call muzzleloaders.

The three primary styles of hunting muzzleloaders today are primitive flintlock, traditional cap lock, and modern style in-line percussion.

THE GUNS

Muzzleloader hunters have one common goal: when the smoke clears, they want to see that their shot was true. It is one thing to own a blackpowder hunting gun. But it's another thing to understand how and why it shoots. Whether you are new to front-end loaders, or a seasoned veteran, lack of preparation does not discriminate. There will be no rewards for the unprepared muzzleloader hunter. This is a one-shot event. Knowledge of the game you hunt, the habitat where they live, and the gun you choose to carry, is essential for success.

The three primary styles of muzzleloading hunting guns of preference today consist of primitive flintlock, traditional caplock, and modern styled in-line ignition percussion. Appearance is not the criteria for a muzzleloading rifle. What matters is how the gun is loaded. Ignition, the manner in which the powder and projectile are discharged from the barrel, is another criterion. The original flintlock was invented in 1670. The first flintlock in-line ignitions were first recorded as long ago as 1738. The invention of the reliable percussion cap in 1807 began the decline in the use of exposed priming powder for ignition. And the first hammerless in-line percussion ignition was patented way back in 1839. Whereas primitive hunters prefer buckhorn rear sights and a front blade, many traditional hunters like a peep sight and front bead or fiber optic sights. Most modern style muzzleloading hunters prefer scopes on their rifles. But let's not overlook that the first telescopes were in use in the early 1600s, and hunting scopes were in the picture by the early 1800s.

IGNITION SYSTEMS

The flintlock is a simple and dependable device when maintained. A piece of sharpened flint is held in the jaws of the hammer. When the trigger is pulled, the hammer falls forward, and the flint strikes a slightly-cupped, vertical piece of steel called the frizzen. As it rocks backward under the flint's blow, it produces a shower of sparks that fall into a flash pan below. The half-full flash pan contains fine FFFFg priming blackpowder that ignites, sending a flame through a flash hole in the side of the barrel and igniting the main charge behind a projectile. The flintlock requires a hands-on, attention-to-detail approach for consistent ignition.

In the caplock–usually considered an improvement over the flintlock–the percussion cap sits on a nipple and contains a small charge of fulminate of mercury, which detonates when struck by the falling hammer. Flame from the cap travels through the nipple and a flash channel to the main barrel charge. The elimination of flint, flashpan, and priming maintenance was very appealing because the new percussion ignition was more tolerant of the weather elements and human error.

Percussion remains the favorite ignition by far in the hammer-style, traditional-looking caplock and in-line percussion-ignited arm. The caplock's nipple is on the side of the barrel of traditional muzzleloaders. The in-line muzzleloader has a nipple set into a breech plug, directly in front of the hammer, and in-line with the barrel. The classic #11 percussion cap sees the widest use today with traditional muzzleloader rifle and shotgun shooters. Musket caps, the top hats of percussion ignitions, are larger percussion caps used on large bore muskets that have been adapted for use on smaller percussion guns.

Although easier to handle, musket caps are no competition for the modern 209-shotgun primer, which has taken center stage today as the primary ignition source for the in-line plunger, bolt-action, drop-action, and break-open percussion rifles and shotguns. Availability, a hot flame for optimum ignition, and a lacquer finish for waterproofing are the reason why the 209 is the top choice today by hunters.

BORE PREPARATION

It doesn't matter what style of muzzleloader you are shooting, if you haven't paid attention to bore condition, you're in trouble. Before the powder and projectile can be loaded, the bore and breech must be clean and dry. The best way to accomplish this is to place a clean, dry patch over a wire brush on your cleaning rod and wipe the bore clean of any moisture, oil, or fouling. Flintlock shooters can wipe the vent hole with a pipe cleaner. Traditional percussion shooters can snap a couple of percussion caps to clear the flash channel. A practice used in modern in-lines is to run another clean patch down to the breech and then snap a primer. This way not only shows that the ignition port is clear but removes all cap or primer fouling as well. Bore preparation is essential for positive ignition, seating a projectile, and achieving accuracy.

PROPELLANTS

Muzzleloaders can be fired only with blackpowder or replica blackpowders. Blackpowder is available in several granulations ranging from coarse to fine. Fineness is denoted by granulation. The ones most often used in shooting muzzleloading firearms are FFg, FFFg, and FFFFg, with the latter being the finest. FFFFg is used only for flintlock priming. FFg and FFFg granulations are used for muzzleloading rifles. The finer FFFg creates higher pressures and is primarily used for smallbore calibers up to .45, and for lighter loads in .50 and .54. Blackpowder is measured in "grains." Most modern blackpowder is manufactured by Goex.

Replica blackpowders weigh substantially less than real blackpowder, so they are loaded by volume, not by weight. This may seem confusing to smokeless powder reloaders who are accustomed to weighing their powder charges. Replica blackpowder charges are measured by how much space they take up, i.e., their volume, not by their weight. In other words, if a powder measure holds

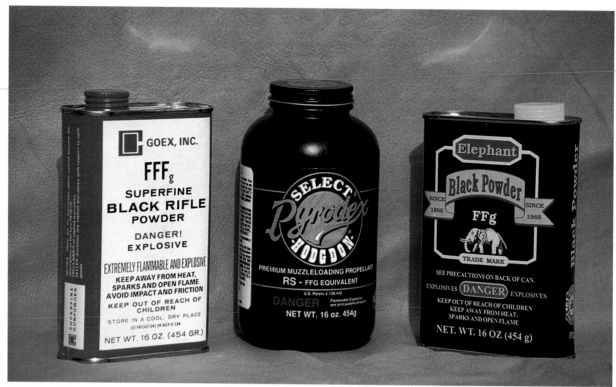

Blackpowder and blackpowder replicas are the only propellants for "Blackpowder Only" firearms.

exactly 70 grains of blackpowder, then this same measure will yield the correct replica blackpowder charge when full. The weight of the charge has nothing to do with it.

Pyrodex by Hodgdon is the most widely accepted replica blackpowder. It is available in granulations ranging from the finest ("P") for pistol (equivalent to FFFG), to "RS" for rifle and shotgun (equivalent to FFG), and the uniform granulation of "Select," strictly quality-controlled for optimum performance and accuracy. Pyrodex P, RS and Select are to be loaded "volume for volume" with the corresponding blackpowder granulation.

Replica blackpowders are popular because they are not as volatile as genuine blackpowder, which means that they are more easily handled, stored, and inventoried. They also tend not to foul as badly as blackpowder does, and post-shooting cleanup is generally easier. However, replica blackpowders do not ignite quite as readily as genuine blackpowder does, and many experienced hunters use hot caps or primers when using them. The 209 shotgun primer, for example, will reliably ignite replica blackpowders.

A relatively recent innovation, the Pyrodex Pellet, has really caught on with in-line shooters. Each pellet, available in 30- or 50- grain charges, is actually a duplex load of 50 grains of RS, with an accelerant on one end that is to be loaded toward the breech. Each Pellet has a hole running its length to enhance ignition.

Hodgdon's latest introduction, "Triple Seven," is already becoming the powder of choice. In loose-powder and "Pellet" form, this new sulfur-free, odorless replica blackpowder produces the boom and smoke of a muzzleloader without the rotten-egg smell and cleans up easily with just plain water. Triple Seven Pellets were designed for use with 209 shotgun primers.

NOTE: Never handle or pour blackpowder or blackpowder replica powders from a bulk container while firing your muzzleloader in the field or at the range. USE A POWDER MEASURE! And always close your box of pellets before firing your gun!

PROJECTILES & RIFLING

Choice of projectiles is governed by a) personal preference, and b) the twist of the rifling in your muzzleloader's barrel. But big game hunting projectiles are also governed by the regulations of the state in which you are muzzleloader hunting. There are three major types of projectiles today: round ball, lead conical, and sabot bullets.

The round ball is guided by a patch that conforms to the rifling and seals ignition gases. The conical is guided by either oversized bands around the bullet that grip the rifling when loading or by a base that obdurates (expands) upon ignition and engages the rifling. The sabot, a cylindrical plastic "case" that hold an undersized bullet, serves the same purpose as the cloth patch: sealing the gases, guiding the smaller bullet through the rifling, and falling away once free of the barrel. Lubrication is imperative for patched round balls, lead conical, and sabots to ease loading and promote consistent accuracy.

Rifling, a series of spiral grooves cut or pressed into a barrel's bore, makes the projectile spin and thus retain

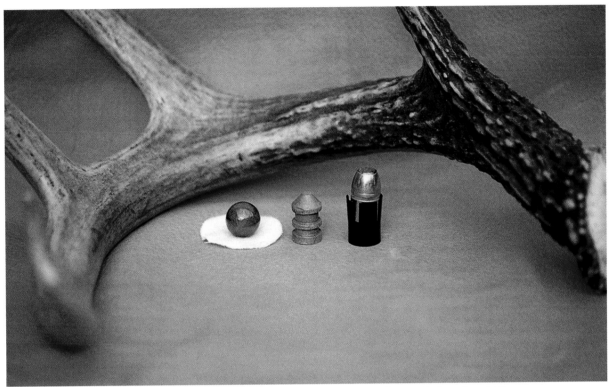

The three major rifle projectiles are the patched round ball, the lead slug, and the sabot bullet.

its stability and accuracy. Rifling twist is expressed as the relationship between number of turns of the projectile in a given length of barrel. A 1:48 rifling twist, for example, will spin the bullet one complete revolution in every 48 inches of barrel length.

Longer projectiles require faster twists. Fast twists such as 1:32, with shallow .006 rifling, work best with lead conical bullets and sabot bullets. Slow twists such as 1:60,with deep .012 rifling, are best suited for patched round balls. The 1:48 inch splits the difference and usually gives acceptable accuracy with both round balls and conicals.

Twist rate is important. In the 1980s Thompson/Center Arms introduced a sporterized, traditionally-styled half-stock carbine that featured a short barrel and a rubber butt on the stock instead of the traditional crescent butt plate. The White Mountain Carbine also featured a 1:20 rate of twist in its rifled barrel. Hunters, though, were still in a patched round ball/slow-twist state of mind. The White Mountain Carbine was intended to perform well with elongated lead conical bullets, not patched round balls that would skip right over the fast twist rifling. But shooters were slow to grasp this then-new concept, which nowadays is taken for granted.

Every once in a while when trying loads at the range you'll get a surprise. For example, my 1:60 inch twist custom round ball rifle shoots a slug that has the same point of impact at 50 yards as it does at 100 yards. It seemingly has a unique S-shaped trajectory that starts when it drops out of the barrel, hits right on at 50 yards, rises high at 75

yards and right back on at 100 yards. But I would have never known this unless I took time to test my gun at the shooting range.

SIGHTING-IN

Marksmanship is the ability to hit your target. Safety and self-confidence are the byproducts of this achievement. As ethical and responsible sportsman, we owe this to the game we hunt. Shooting excellence depends on fundamental techniques that need to be learned and practiced. They include shooting position, aiming, trigger squeeze, breath control and follow-through. Whether you are standing on the ground or sitting in a treestand, you still need your pins under you for a steady aim. But, before you can practice marksmanship afield, you need a muzzleloader that has been put through the paces at the shooting range from a stable bench-rest.

Sighting-in should start at close range for two reasons. First, if your muzzleloader is very far off its mark, the shorter distance will keep your shots within a smaller, easy to determine area. Secondly, there is what is known as the 13-yard rule. This is based on the trajectory of the average muzzleloading rifle. When sighting-in at 13 yards, your gun will be a bit high at 50 yards, almost right on at 75 yards, and a bit low at 100. This is an effective way to take the frustration out the initial sighting in of a muzzleloading rifle. By getting the gun grouping at close range, you only need to fine tune the gun at longer ranges. Sight adjustments for primitive rifles will include drifting the rear sight left or right and filing the front sight for eleva-

Only a stable bench rest will allow you to accurately sight-in your rifle.

tion. The generation of sporterized caplocks with adjustable ramp sights, peep sights, and now fiber-optics have made the sighting-in process easier. A properly mounted, light-gathering scope with accurate click adjustments is the most efficient form of sighting-in to date.

Choosing a load has come a long way in the last 30 years. Most manufacturers provide a manual with suggested loads for their muzzleloaders. The best load is not always the most powerful one. By starting with your manufacturer's suggested low-end load, shoot a three-shot group at 13 yards. Adjust your sights and move the group where you want it to be on the target. Then move out to 50 yards and repeat the process. Incrementally increase your charge until your group begins to open up. Then back it down until you achieve your tightest groups. Only then, with the rifle zeroed in with an optimum load should you can proceed to test your limits at longer ranges. Stay within your manufacturer's guidelines. Once you've sighted in your gun on a bench rest, practice offhand. Offhand shooting may very well determine the success or failure of your hunt.

EFFECTIVE RANGE

Era, interest and purpose afield should be your muzzleloading big game guide. The killing power of a muzzleloader is definitely adequate for deer when used within the effective limits of both the hunter, and gun in hand. The 50-caliber has proven itself to be the most versatile caliber by maintaining its velocity and energy with various projectiles. The most common big game calibers are .45, .50, and .54, with the latter two the most prevalent. The .50 round ball can be an excellent shooter, as I have produced some wonderful targets with both flintlock and percussion guns. But in the hunting woods, my 50-caliber flintlock's proven round ball deer load is 70 grains of FFFg Elephant Brand Blackpowder. This load pushes the 177-grain spherical projectile at 1800 feet per second (velocity), and produces 1300 foot-pounds of energy at the muzzle. But the energy dwindles to just over 400 fpe at 100 yards. Shooting offhand with the primitive sights on this gun, my flintlock and I need to be within 50 yards of a deer.

My 54-caliber custom percussion sidehammer handles a stout powder charge and lead slug worthy of the mountain men and buffalo hunters of yesterday. 100 grains of

The effective limits of both the hunter, and the gun in hand, will determine the success or failure of the shot.

Goex blackpowder delivers a 430-grain Thompson/Center Maxi-Ball (lead slug) at just over 1300 fps, with over 1600 fpe at the muzzle. At 100 yards, the slug still has over 1000 fpe, but dwindles rapidly after that. This load has performed solidly on big game. The peep sight and front bead on this rifle make it a hard-hitting 100-yard gun.

A .50 caliber Knight scoped in-line modern rifle I shoot takes a back seat to no one. One hundred and twenty grains of Pyrodex Select pushing a 45-caliber 250-grain Barnes copper-jacketed bullet in a sabot produces 1800 fps and 1800 fpe at the muzzle. At 100 yards, the flat shooting load still has 1000 fpe. When compared to the rainbow trajectories of the round ball and heavy slug, this combination in this rifle makes it a worthy load at 150 yards for big game and varmints.

By taking the time to properly sight in and learn your muzzleloading rifle's preferences off a stationary rest, and then shooting at progressive yardages to determine your offhand effective range, you can approach your hunting season with realistic and knowledgeable shooting expectations.

SIMPLE FOR SUCCESS

Keep your field accessories simple when hunting. You need a priming device, a capper or pan charger, and carry an extra flint or nipple. Today's speed loaders are an excellent and safe way to pack your pre-measured charges and projectiles. A short starter to get the lubricated projectile introduced to the barrel. Other accessories should include a vent pick and pan brush for the flintlock, a nipple pick and nipple wrench for percussion, and ramrod accessories such as a cleaning jag and ball puller for the unexpected. These items can be carried in a small, unobtrusive belt mounted shooting bag, your toolbox afield.

The ramrod was the original muzzleloading accessory for maintenance and loading. It is just as important today. I always carry and use a wire cleaning brush for all my patchwork because of its better bore fit and patch purchase. For hunting, I strongly recommend a synthetic, flexible ramrod, as they are much more forgiving when the adrenaline is flowing. And please, mark your ramrod at both the empty and loaded positions. This will instantly tell if the muzzleloader is loaded, and if so, loaded right.

It's the lucky hunter that bags the record book buck. But the quality of a muzzleloader hunt does not have to be determined by antler size alone.

ACCEPT THE CHALLENGE

The creation of a hunting load, one step at a time, down the barrel of your rifle, is why it is called muzzleloading. The only way you can become a competent and confident shooter is by becoming acquainted with your firearm and knowledgeable of the elements of primitive shooting. We are living in a time when there have never been more muzzleloader hunting opportunities for sportsman to participate in, with specific muzzleloader seasons throughout the United States and Canada. As a Field Editor for *Blackpowder Hunting* magazine, the official publication of the International Blackpowder Hunting Association, I think that it's evident, by the sheer variety of articles in each issue, that muzzleloader hunting is not only alive and well in North America, but popular around the free world. The National Muzzle Loading Rifle Association was formed in 1933 and continues to support all historical, shooting and hunting aspects of muzzleloading. The NMLRA also maintains the Longhunter Big Game Records Program. A look through the leather-bound volume honoring the 32 big game species lets one know that muzzleloader big game hunting is as popular as ever and that game management programs have paid off with thriving populations of big game animals. Muzzleloader hunting is not complicated. It is just a single-shot state of mind. Knowing the traits, habits, and habitat of your intended game is the key to putting yourself in the position for muzzleloader success. Muzzleloader hunters today, although pressed by the demands of modern living, will find their days afield more productive and enjoyable by being knowledgeable of both their game and gun.

2

The Boom In Muzzleloader Hunting

BLACKPOWDER PROPELLANTS

Gunpowder is gunpowder, right? Wrong! Each propellant has a purpose that is right for specific shooting and hunting needs. For many, their first exposure to blackpowder was viewing a gala Fourth of July celebration, with spectacular starbursts in the sky and the concussions of the large explosions that created them. My first was going to a North-South Skirmish Association mortar and cannon competition back in the mid-1960s. Their tremendous muzzle flashes and billowing clouds of white smoke fascinated me. Today, many collectors and hunters are turning to this primitive propellant for their favorite firearm of an earlier era.

Blackpowder is the fuel for muzzleloading rifles and shotguns. This ancient formulation is a mixture of saltpeter (potassium nitrate), charcoal and sulfur. The right components and their proper ratio for ignition took centuries to develop. Think of the attrition rate of people attempting to create the proper mixture of 75 parts saltpeter, 15 parts charcoal, and 10 parts sulfur. The saltpeter is the oxidizer, or contributor of the oxygen needed for combustion; the charcoal, the body of the propellant; and the sulfur, the binding agent. Those proportions were discovered in 1751, and they are still the standard today.

Blackpowder is a Class A Explosive that should be handled with common sense and stored in a safe place. Blackpowder ignites rapidly but burns slowly, as it is a "surface burning" propellant. Because of this, blackpowder is created in the form of grains, the size and resulting surface area of which determine the rate of burn. The finer the granulation, the faster the rate of burn. Although blackpowder can achieve high pressures, it is considered a low-yield propellant when compared to modern smoke-

Smokeless powder is NEVER to be used in Blackpowder Only firearms.

less powders. After all, it was developed for shooting implements with open ignition ports. Blowback from too high a pressure would not be desirable.

As mentioned in the last chapter, volumetric loading of blackpowder is acceptable and safe with muzzleloaders because it is not as efficient as smokeless powder. For example, it takes only 30 grains of smokeless powder to propel a 170-grain, 30-30 bullet at about 2200 fps. It takes 120 grains of an FFg granulation of blackpowder to push a 230 grain round ball at about 2000 fps muzzle velocity. Because of their faster burn rate and higher pressures, smokeless powders are NEVER to be substituted in any blackpowder firearms.

Today, the most prominent name in blackpowder is Goex. Goex has been made in America since 1812. The Goex plant in Doyline, La., is the only blackpowder producer in the Americas. Elephant Blackpowder, made in Brazil, had been produced since 1866 until it went out of production a few years ago. Schuetzen Black Powder and

Blackpowder ignites rapidly but burns slowly.

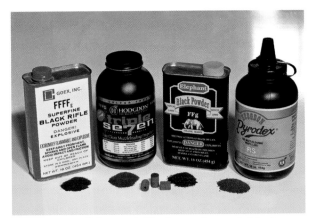

The most widely used blackpowder and blackpowder substitutes to date have been produced by Goex, Elephant and Hodgdon.

FFFFg blackpowder is for flintlock priming only.

Swiss Black Powder are imports that are relatively new to U.S. shooters. Schuetzen, Swiss and Elephant blackpowder are distributed by Schuetzen Powder, LCC, of Arlington, Texas.

Blackpowder is sold in one-pound cans that consist of 7000 grains of powder. Granulations range from a very coarse grade for cannons to very fine granules for flintlock priming pans. Although made from the same ingredients, the coarse granulations burn the slowest and perform best in the larger fusils (large-bore shoulder arms, usually smoothbores), with the faster burning fine powder working best in the small caliber rifles and pistols. The granule sizes include Fg for large bore 75-caliber or 10-gauge muskets; FFg, which performs best in medium-bore muzzleloaders from about 58-caliber down to 45-caliber; FFFg, for 45-caliber and smaller muzzleloaders and most blackpowder pistols; and FFFFg, for flintlock priming only. Specialty granulations include a Cartridge grade for breech-loading blackpowder cartridge arms and a Cannon grade for full-size cannon and mortars.

An inherent trait of blackpowder is the cloud of white smoke it produces. This is a direct result of the inefficient conversion of blackpowder (a solid) into blackpowder gas. The finer-grain powders are consumed more efficiently upon ignition than coarser-grained powders. The cloud of smoke is the visual effect of blackpowder ignition. What you don't see is the partially burned residue coating the inside of your barrel. This is called fouling, the bane of all blackpowder enthusiasts. Unattended fouling increases bore pressures, which is noticeable in the form of a decline in accuracy. Newcomers to muzzleloading soon confront the necessity of wiping the bore clean as their projectiles become more difficult to load. If left in the bore, fouling may also contaminate and weaken a fresh charge of powder. Fouling is also extremely hygroscopic (water-attracting), and it can cause irreversible rusting of a gun's bore in a matter of days, if not sooner.

Since blackpowder is not measured by weight as is smokeless powder, volumetric measuring is the standard

The granulation of blackpowder determines its rate of burn.

for blackpowder charges. Small variances in volume are not critical, so volumetric blackpowder measures operate in increments of 5 and 10 grains. A few grains more or less seems to make no detectable difference in the performance of a muzzleloader.

Pyrodex, probably the most popular blackpowder substitute or replica, is manufactured by the Hodgdon Powder Company of Shawnee Mission, Kan., and entered the world of muzzleloading in 1976. It comes in a variety of granulations, which produce very similar pressures and velocities. Whereas blackpowder is classified a Class A explosive with strict guidelines for storage and sales, Pyrodex is a Class B flammable solid, just as are modern smokeless powders. Pyrodex, like blackpowder, is made in different granulations for different shooting applications. Pyrodex grades include P for pistols and small bore rifles, RS for rifles and shotguns, and SELECT, which is a premium RS that is specially processed and tested. For the blackpowder breechloader cartridge there is CTG. Pyrodex is to be loaded volume for volume, not weight, when substituted for blackpowder. For example, 100 grains of FFg blackpowder equals only 70.5 grains of RS at the same setting on a volumetric measure. Pyrodex also tends to produce less fouling than blackpowder, though it doesn't remove the need for regular bore cleaning.

Unattended fouling will increase bore pressures.

Blackpowder and blackpowder substitutes are powerful propellants deserving the utmost respect.

An innovative Pyrodex entry is the Pyrodex Pellet, which is RS compressed into 30-, 50-, and 60-grain pellets with one end coated with a sensitive ignition compound. The new pellets are designed to perform in the modern in-line percussion rifles. These preformed, pre-measured charges are consistent by nature, convenient to handle, and easy to load: just drop 'em down the barrel with the ignition end down. A hole running the length of the pellet enhances percussion ignition. Hodgdon's latest creation, Triple Seven, is a non-sulfur, great shooting, easy cleaning, replica blackpowder that is available in both granule and pellet form.

Goex's replica product is called Clear Shot. This blackpowder substitute is also classified as a Class B flammable solid for easier shipping and handling. Clear Shot has also proven to be less corrosive while producing virtually identical velocities when compared with blackpowder. Clear Shot, like Pyrodex, should be loaded volume for volume, exactly like blackpowder. American Pioneer Powder is a new replica powder available in granular, pre-measured loads and compressed charges and also features no-sulfur smell and easy cleanup.

Both blackpowder and the above-mentioned substitutes have their pros and cons. Blackpowder ignites more easily, which makes it the only choice for use with a flint-

Whether shooting a solid projectile or birdshot, make certain every load is seated correctly.

Blackpowder–not a replica blackpowder–is the best choice for the flintlock hunter.

lock muzzleloader. The barrel charge of a flintlock needs to be FFg or FFFg, with the pan powder FFFFg. Some back-hammer caplocks with snail or barrel style ignition ports that house the nipple often show a preference for the hotter ignition of blackpowder. Most traditional muzzleloading enthusiasts prefer the original propellant, blackpowder.

Pyrodex and Triple Seven shoot as well as blackpowder and burn cleaner. But they require an efficient percussion ignition system. For example, I have a traditional side-hammer (also called a "mule-ear") of authentic mid-1800s styling. The nipple is mounted directly on the side, perpendicular to the barrel, and the spring-like hammer slaps it to fire the cap. The percussion cap flash goes directly to the charge with no angles or obstacles to contend with. This lets the gun perform well with either blackpowder or Pyrodex, much like the modern styled in-lines. Pyrodex works fine in blackpowder guns with adequate flash to the barrel charge. Today, the most common percussion ignition sources are the traditional #11 percussion cap, the easy to handle and larger musket cap, and the in-line ignition favorite, the #209 shotgun primer.

As previously mentioned, blackpowder doesn't burn clean. A feature of Pyrodex is that the fouling after a shot is reduced. It is greatly reduced with sulfur-free Triple Seven. Due to this, many shots can be loaded in succes-

sion. Although several shots can be loaded in succession, proper cleaning is required after each shooting session whether it is good old-fashioned hot, soapy water or a modern cleaning solvent.

Obtaining proper blackpowder loads for blackpowder firearms is easier today than ever before. Manufacturers provide loading manuals to guide you to safe and accurate shooting. These manuals start with a minimum load for sighting in, then feature an optimum and maximum load. For example, Thompson/Center's loading manual for 50-caliber round ball loads starts at 50 grains of FFg, shows an optimum performance load at 80 grains FFg, and cites a maximum load 110 grains of FFg. Blackpowder and its replicas rather quickly reach a point of diminishing returns, where adding more powder does nothing more than create more boom and kick without achieving any more velocity. Stay within your gunmaker's loading guidelines. And for safety and accuracy, learn to seat every load with equal pressure. Gun, powder, and projectile manufacturers now offer loading charts showing the best load for each projectile along with their trajectories and downrange velocities and sustained energy.

Due to the burning rate of primitive propellants, the debate of barrel length often arises. Just look at the muzzle blast of any Pyrodex or blackpowder loaded gun to see the incomplete combustion in action. A 36-caliber rifle I

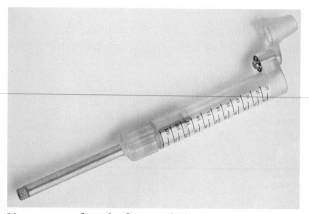

Never pour directly from a bulk container. USE A POWDER MEASURE.

own with a 39-inch barrel produces over 2000 fps with a 40-grain load of FFFg. The same load in a 28-inch barrel produces 1800 fps. Yes, the longer barrel helps with better powder combustion. But is it worth the tradeoff in length and weight, especially in a hunting gun? Some say yes, some say no, but that extra 11 inches of iron is going to feel pretty heavy at the end of the day.

When creating your load with the main ingredients of powder and projectile, remember the rules of safe loading and handling:

1) Never use smokeless powder in a gun labeled black powder only.

2) Never pour powder directly from a bulk container. Use a powder measure.

3) Treat every gun as if it is loaded.

4) Keep the muzzle angled away from head and body when loading.

5) Make certain that every load is seated correctly. (Mark your ramrod depth to show both loaded and unloaded points to remove any doubt. A short-started or unseated load can have disastrous results.)

6) If a misfire occurs, KEEP THE FIREARM POINTED DOWNRANGE. After one minute, clean out the ignition port, prime and try again. If this does not work after several attempts, pull the charge with a screw-type ball puller and start over.

Pyrodex, Triple Seven and their predecessor, blackpowder, are powerful propellants deserving the utmost respect in both handling and shooting. Knowledge is the key to respecting the properties of these propellants and the firearms that use them. Each granulation has a specific purpose for safe and efficient use in a muzzleloading firearm. With the proper powder to match your gun, it won't take long to find the load that best meets your blackpowder hunting needs.

(For in-depth reading try *The Complete Blackpowder Handbook*, 4th edition, by Sam Fadala/K-P Books.)

The following should be read and understood by every shooter, no matter his or her age.

MUZZLELOADING CAUTIONS & COMMANDMENTS
Courtesy: Dixie Gun Works, Inc.

1) USE ONLY BLACKPOWDER OR REPLICA BLACKPOWDER IN MUZZLELOADERS. Pyrodex is the brand name of the most commonly known replica black powder.

2) TREAT EVERY GUN AS LOADED. Never point it at anything you don't intend to shoot. Keep the muzzle pointed in a safe direction at all times, including while loading. Never lean over the muzzle. Make priming the pan or capping the nipple the last step in loading.

3) BE SURE OF YOUR TARGET BEFORE FIRING. Be aware of the location of other people around you. Know what is behind your target. Never fire into water or flat, hard surfaces. Round balls are prone to glance or ricochet.

4) BE SURE YOUR GUN IS IN FIRING CONDITION BEFORE YOU PULL THE TRIGGER. Make sure the ball is firmly seated, the gun is not overcharged, there is no obstruction in the barrel, etc.

5) TREAT A MISFIRE OR FAILURE TO FIRE WITH EXTREME CARE. Keep the gun pointed in a safe direction down range, and wait at least one full minute before re-priming.

6) MAKE SURE YOUR GUN IS UNLOADED BEFORE YOU STORE IT. STORE THE GUN, POWDER, AND CAPS SEPARATELY.

7) PROTECT YOUR EYES AND EARS WHILE SHOOTING. Always wear shooting glasses and ear protection to prevent possible damage.

8) NEVER SMOKE WHILE LOADING, SHOOTING, OR HANDLING BLACKPOWDER PROPELLANTS.

9) NEVER DRINK ALCOHOLIC BEVERAGES BEFORE OR WHILE SHOOTING.

10) USE COMMON SENSE AT ALL TIMES.

BARREL PRESSURES AND SAFETY

Blackpowder does more than just go boom. Understanding the propellant's pressure in relation to bore size is imperative for safety, velocity, and accuracy. A cap-'n'-ball .44 revolver that has a maximum load of 40 grains of FFFg or Pyrodex P may perform accurately only with 25 grains of powder with a cornmeal buffer to fill the cylinder. The additional powder would only create more boom from the volume and more recoil from the pressure. Neither of these traits is desirable in the short sidearm.

Finer granulations of blackpowder burn faster than the coarse. Shooting small caliber rifles is what really illustrates why so little powder is needed in the small bores. As previously mentioned, a .36 rifle using 40 grains of FFFg fires its small projectile at 2000 fps. The finer powder burning in the smaller bore provides less space for the expanding gases from the burning powder to work in. A 5-grain increase in a powder charge can significantly increase the small bore's barrel pressure and subsequent velocity. Smallbores are more sensitive to load variation than the bigger caliber muzzleloaders.

In contrast, a 62-caliber flintlock I have shoots almost twice the powder charge of the .36 with 70 grains of FFFg. But it produces a velocity of around only 1100 fps, the reason being that the larger bore has more space for the expanding gases to work, thus lowering barrel pressures. Manufacturers' suggested loads have been pretested to provide safe and accurate performance. Too little powder will result in a rainbow trajectory and poor accuracy. Too much powder will push the safety envelope and also diminish accuracy as well. My 54-caliber rifle shooting a hefty 100-grain charge of Pyrodex Select pushes a round ball along at over 1500 fps. This is a proper powder granulation as it produces barrel pressures well within safety limits while producing cloverleaf target accuracy.

How does the thin-walled shotgun fare in barrel pressure and bore size? For starters, shotguns shoot Pyrodex RS, or blackpowder in FFg. Shotguns larger than 10 gauge use the Fg granulation. A stiff 12-gauge turkey load of 100 grains of FFg pushing 1 1/2-ounces of shot will produce less than 1200 fps velocity, the reason being the slower-burning, larger kernels of FFg in a bigger bore. Bigger bores render far less pressure per powder charge and granulation than the smaller bore because the larger bore has a greater volume for gas pressure to disperse in. Thus, larger powder charges of the appropriate granulations are used for effective hunting loads.

The one thing that the barrel pressures of any blackpowder shooting iron will not tolerate is a short-started (unseated) load in which the ball is not firmly seated on the powder. Though the phenomenon is not well understood, it appears that the air space created by an unseated load causes the powder to detonate rather than burn. That is not good. For safety's sake, use the manufacturers' suggested powder granulation and suggested loads and make certain every powder/ projectile combination is seated correctly.

3

Enhancing, Loading, Maintaining, and Accessorizing Your Muzzleloader

THE BARREL

The word "muzzleloader" perfectly describes blackpowder hunting guns. Everything begins with the muzzle, the business end of the gun. Breech plugs, ignition ports, trigger assembly, lock mechanism, barrel keys and pins, barrel sights, sling swivel barrel thimbles, and ram-rods–all of these depend on the barrel, the heart of a muzzle-loader. Early barrels were made by pounding steel strips around pipe and welding the seams. By 1840, barrels were rendered from cast steel ingots converted into round, square, and octagon bars of various lengths. In the 1850s gun-barrel iron was developed by compressing malleable cast ingots. Hydraulic presses removed "blow holes" or flaws in the metal, giving a finer-grain, stronger, and more homogenous barrel steel than ever before.

DESIGN & FUNCTION

The "boom" in muzzleloading starts in the breech of the barrel with the pull of a trigger. Single triggers, double-set triggers, or adjustable triggers release the firing mechanism–which may be a hammer, a striker, or a slapper–on a muzzleloader. Double-set triggers on traditional flintlock and percussion guns have been the standard. By setting the rear trigger (or "set trigger"), the adjustable front trigger can then be released with little pressure, enhancing shooter accuracy. The single trigger became popular as more and more shooters used their muzzleloaders primarily for hunting rather than targets.

R.E. Davis Company of Perrysburg, Ohio, makes fine replacement triggers, single and double, their popular model being the "Davis Deerslayer." Davis triggers fit most traditional-style muzzleloaders and are easily installed. Many modern-style muzzleloaders feature adjustable triggers that let the gun react as if it were part of you, a feature

Every part of this muzzleloading rifle, even the shooter, contributes to barrel function.

The boom in muzzleloading starts in the breech of the barrel at the pull of a trigger.

that certainly enhances target shooting and hunting shots taken at longer ranges.

The flintlock's flash first ignited barrel charges around

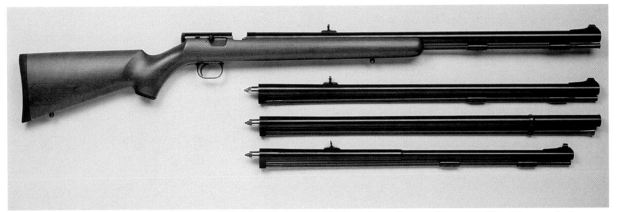

This Thompson/Center System 1 rifle features interchangeable barrels in large caliber, small caliber, and shotgun.

Gunstocks like this laminated (top) and custom curly maple with inlays (bottom) are two styles that cradle today's muzzleloading barrels.

1615 and was popular for the next two hundred years. The percussion cap gained popularity after 1807. The traditional caplock was the most popular muzzleloading ignition mechanism until Tony Knight's in-line striker ignition gained popularity in the 1980s. Modern style front-stuffers with removable breech plugs have become phenomenally popular during the last decade as more deer and turkey hunters have taken advantage of special seasons.

In a muzzleloader, a charge of blackpowder and a projectile–in that order, mind you–are loaded through the muzzle and are firmly seated with a ramrod. The performance of a muzzleloading rifle projectile is influenced by the rate of rifling twist and the depth of the rifling grooves cut into the bore. The pattern density of the pellets in a muzzleloading shot charge is influenced by a constriction at the muzzle called the choke. Early smoothbores were very popular because the one-gun hunter could shoot both shot and patched round ball, although roundball accuracy could be a little iffy. Today, shotgun barrels with interchangeable chokes meet the demands of wing-shooters and upland game and wild turkey hunters alike.

In the early- to mid-nineteenth century, rifled barrels became popular for solid projectiles because of their superior accuracy. Today, we know that shallow, fast twist

rifling of 1:20 to 1:48 is compatible with elongated slugs or sabot bullets. Slower, deeper twists exceeding 1:60 perform best with the highly accurate patched round ball. Modern muzzleloading barrels have taken a modular approach in which interchangeable barrels are available for many front-stuffers. For example, with your favorite muzzleloader today you could interchange a 32-caliber barrel for small game, a 50-caliber barrel for big game, and a 12-gauge shotgun for turkeys and upland game. Single-shot muzzleloading barrels are even available for modern pump shotguns such as the Mossberg 500!

Stocks may be wood, laminates, or synthetics in full-length, half-stock, and thumbhole styles. There is nothing more handsome than a beautiful curly maple, full-length stock on a hand-made traditional style muzzleloader. Both of my custom-made rifles feature beautifully figured wood. But modern-style, synthetic-stocked muzzleloaders seem to sell better than their wood-stocked counterparts, especially to the once-a-year special season hunter. Many of these synthetic stocks also feature recoil pads and Monte Carlo styling to help tame stout recoil.

The styling of a particular gun, of course, has no bearing on terminal performance. A 26-inch 50-caliber barrel with a 1:28 rate of twist loaded with 100 grains of blackpowder and a 370-grain lead slug will produce given ballistics, measured in feet per second and foot pounds of energy, regardless of what style muzzleloading gun, stock, or ignition it was fired from.

SIGHTS

The first barrel sights were a fixed protrusion on the top of the end of the tube. Next came the addition of a rear sight. The realization grew that a longer barrel that separated the sights by a greater distance resulted in improved aiming–hence the traditional "long rifles." By the early nineteenth century, the dovetailed buckhorn rear and fixed blade front sight came into vogue. To adjust windage, you tapped the rear sight to one side or the other in its dovetail cut. To adjust elevation, you filed the front sight–but not too much! Barrel sights further advanced with the onset of adjustable rear sights. In the constant

Fiber optic sights improve visibility against any background.

search for more accurate sights for long-distance shooting, receiver mounted sights such as the Vernier tang became the sharpshooter's friend.

Another receiver sight was the low profile peep. It became very popular with deer hunters because the front post naturally centers in the peep for quick, accurate shooting. Lyman Products Corporation is known today for its excellent muzzleloading rifles and accessories. Formed in 1878 by William Lyman, the Lyman Gun Sight Company soon introduced its popular No. 1 tang sight, patented in 1879. The original Lyman sight used an aperture or peep sight close to the eye.

As is true of so many good ideas, the principle was nothing new. Peep sights are actually older than the rifle. Some medieval crossbows had peep sights. But William Lyman designed a peep sight that was universally accepted by shooters. Previously, target peep sights had so small a hole that finding a target while looking through it was difficult. William discovered that the hole could be much larger because the eye naturally centers the hole without any conscious effort. Shooters could now see the landscape through the Lyman peep and quickly find their target or a running deer.

Front sights had seen little attention by existing gun companies until William Lyman discovered that a small bead of ivory stood out against a dark forest background

Scopes, peeps, and open shotgun sights all contribute to accurate shooting.

exceptionally well when compared to the black iron sights of the day. One story says that William made a trip to the Adirondack Mountains where he had heard of a local hunter who had fashioned a front sight from a bear's tooth. The yellow-white color was said to show up very well against nearly any background. William expanded on this idea and created a new front sight. After all, he had the perfect material to work with: real ivory. His father David exported mules to the West Indies and had been importing ivory for many years. William designed an ivory plug cutter that fashioned small cylinders of ivory that were placed vertically in a steel front sight base so they protruded high enough to give plenty of reflected light. The resulting Lyman ivory bead front sight for rifles, the predecessor to the fiber optics of today, was patented in 1885.

Nowadays, Lyman, Williams, and Tru-Glo all make excellent receiver, barrel, and front sights. One of the best innovations in open sights for hunters is the fiber optic sight system that really lines up the front and back sights quickly, even under low light conditions. The optical advantage of a scope has its place on muzzleloading guns, too. Bushnell, Simmons, Leupold, Thompson/Center, and BSA scopes have all sat upon rifles and turkey shotguns in my cabinet. There is little question that a good scope gathers light, helps find your target, and contributes to accuracy. An excellent product for leveling a scope is the Reticle Leveler from Segway Industries. This leveler helps the shooter avoid canting (tilting) the barrel to one side or the other, which can throw off an otherwise well-aimed shot.

The Ashley Power Rod has built-in witness marks and a flip out T handle for assertive loading.

FEEDING AND FIRING

Unlike modern guns which involve only the gun and a cartridge, muzzleloaders require a number of components.

Obviously, nothing happens without gunpowder. The proper granulation of Goex blackpowder, Goex Clear Shot, Elephant brand blackpowder, or Hodgdon's Pyrodex or Triple Seven is the power behind the projectile. A fabric patch is used with roundballs to seal barrel gases and guide the ball through the rifling. A felt bore button cushions and seals a lead conical slug. The modern sabot (pronounced "sa-BO" or "SA-bo," from the Old French word for "wooden shoe," believe it or not) acts like a little plastic jacket that carries and guides the sub-caliber projectile, sometimes a modern jacketed bullet, on its journey through the barrel.

Lubricants enhance loading and shooting accuracy. The shotgun wad protects the pellets from deforming while the over-shot card keeps the shot charge intact. To get loading components down the barrel, a short starter introduces the solid projectiles into the bore. The short starter is a short ramrod with a stout palm piece that lets you apply sufficient power to force the projectile into the rifling. Finally, a ramrod seats the lubricated bullet upon the powder charge. The shotgun shooter uses the ramrod twice per load, one for the wad over the powder, and once for the over-shot card.

The ramrod gets a good workout handling both loading and cleaning duties. It didn't take long in my muzzleloading career to discover that wooden ramrods have their

Percussion ignitions today are the #11 percussion cap, the musket cap, and the 209 shotgun primer.

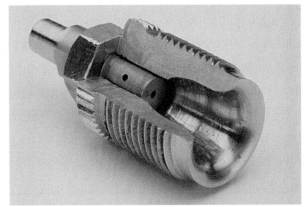

Advanced designs in breech plugs from companies such as Thompson/Center enhance modern percussion ignition.

Lubrication and preservation through thorough cleaning are essential to maintain the rifled or smoothbore barrel, firing mechanism, triggers and breeches of your muzzleloader.

limitations when it comes to loading projectiles down rifled barrels. They break. Then one happy day I stumbled upon Mountain State Muzzleloading's Hunter Super-Rod. These stout synthetic ramrods are custom made to fit any muzzleloader. The Super-Rod has a cleaning jag and concealed ball puller on one end, and a threaded tip on the other to take a bore brush or other accessory.

Ashley Outdoors also offers a superior ramrod in its Ashley Power Rod. The Power Rod is a solid aluminum ramrod that comes in one length or as a segmented takedown rod. The strength of this rod eliminates the short starter when loading projectiles. A built-in T handle flips out to provide real purchase for stuffing that patched ball or snug bullet down the barrel. The Power Rod also has built in "witness marks" for load references. Rod attachments include a ball puller, cleaning jag, and specially-shaped tips for loading hollow point bullets, lead slugs, and round balls. For the truly horrible situation of getting your ramrod stuck at home or in the field, there is Mountain State Muzzleloading's Perfect Puller. This brass fitting gives you significantly better purchase to remove the stuck rod in question.

Improving ignition reliability has been an ongoing crusade in the world of muzzleloading. For the flintlock shooter, Michaels of Oregon offers the Touch Hole Liner. This stainless steel liner has a cone-shaped interior that creates a venturi effect to accelerate the flow of hot gases from the pan to the barrel breech for more reliable igni-

tion of flintlock guns. For percussion guns, the flared-edge musket cap gained acceptance in the 1900's until the 209 shotgun primer took over as the main ignition source for in-line rifles and shotguns. The readily available flame-throwing 209-shotgun primer is now the top seller among in-line rifle and shotgun hunters, the most popular brands being CCI, Federal, Winchester and Cheddite. Advanced designs in breech plugs from companies such as Thompson/Center, CVA, Remington and Knight also enhanced modern percussion ignition.

CCI, RWS, and Remington have all improved their percussion caps. The new Magnum #11 percussion caps are hotter, and when used with improved nipple designs such as Mountain State Muzzleloading's Spit-Fire Magnum Nipple, they will continue to see wide use among traditional muzzleloader rifle and shotgun shooters. Blomquist Percussion Works makes a full line of replacement nipples to improve percussion ignition on all models of traditional and modern rifles.

LUBRICATION & PRESERVATION

Muzzleloading requires two kinds of lubricants: 1) a bullet lube to help the projectile enter and exit the bore, and 2) a gun lubricant to help prevent rust and permit disassembly of the gun.

The patched round ball always requires lubricant. I have used spit, dish soap, Vaseline, Moose Juice, Old Slickum, and natural lubes such as T/C's #13 to get the job

These eight hunting bags carry the efficient loading system and field accessories for whichever approach to muzzleloading you choose. The author's traditional hunting bags include Thompson/Center's smooth leather shoulder bag and camouflage Hunter's Field Pouch (back left), October Country's Couer d'Alene (back center), and the rugged #4 cotton duck Uplander bag from Great Miami Sport Bags (back right). Camouflage bags in front include the Traditions Belt Pack (left) and CVA's Fleece Possibles Bag. The Humber Valley belt pouch and an Uncle Mike's fringed shoulder bag round out the group (front right).

done. Liquid dish soap is preferred by a couple of my rifles and has worked the best for round ball loading and shooting. The lead slug must have a paste lubricant for loading and accurate shooting. Ox-Yoke's Wonder Lube 1000 Plus is an industry standard as a natural lubricant and bore-seasoning agent. But not all barrels like natural lubes. Lubricants are not generally recommended for use with saboted bullets, but without a touch of lubricant, many such bullets would never get loaded. Lubrication is not necessary for loading shotguns, but many shooters prefer lightly-lubed felt cushion wads just under the shot charge.

Good old hot water and soap still get the job done when it comes to cleaning your soot burner. There are now very good products to enhance the cleaning procedure. Dixie Gun Work's Black Solve cleaning solution really gets the gunk out when it comes to swabbing your muzzleloader. It comes in the form of a 4 oz. bottle of liquid concentrate that yields 32 oz. of cleaner. Black Solve is very efficient used on a patch or with a barrel-flushing unit. Ox-Yoke's cleaning kits feature stout cleaning rods, brushes, patches and accessories that are excellent for muzzleloader cleaning duties. Knight's Cleaning Solvent is excellent and removes blackpowder residue quickly and easily.

For the shooter who still prefers to lightly oil his cleaned gun, there are Knight's Oil with rust inhibitor and Crouse's Masking Gun Lubricant from the noted animal lure maker, Pete Rickard Inc. This non-petroleum lubricant comes in masking scents of pine and cedar and is a must for the close-quarters deer hunter. The advent of removable breech plugs has created its own need for hardy lubricants, such as T/C's Gorilla Grease, to ease plug removal after a shooting session. Breech plugs are notorious for seizing up if ignored.

Whichever lube or cleaner you choose, remember that lubrication and preservation are a must in order to maintain an accurate barrel on your muzzleloader.

FIELD ESSENTIALS

Your shooting, sporting or hunting bag is your tool box in the field, and the selection has never been better than it is today. They come small, big, fringed, or furry and range from ornate and large to small and simple. I have amassed eight different bags over the years. My two largest bags are excellent for the shotgun as they contain several compartments to hold powder, wads, shot, and overshot cards along with the other shooting necessities of powder and ignition.

One of my favorite large bags is my October Country Couer d'Alene. It is a beautiful leather shoulder bag with scalloped suede-edged flap with traditional red wool weeping-heart stitching. My other large bag is from Dixie Gun Works and is made by Great Miami Sport Bags. This rugged #4 cotton duck bag is very handsome in a design called the Uplander, and it's a very functional field companion for the traditional hunter.

My medium-size bags include my original fringed shoulder bag from Uncle Mike's; a simple, smooth leather shoulder bag from Thompson/Center; a lightweight, dual-compartment, camouflage belt pack from Traditions; and CVA's fleece possibles bag with numerous inside and outside compartments, with a carrying strap that can be worn over the shoulder or at the waist.

I also use two small bags quite often. One is an old Humber Valley leather belt bag with weeping heart in a beaver tail design flap. The other is Thompson/Center's camouflaged Hunter's Field Pouch. These are great for a few speed loaders, ignition source, and basic field essentials. Both styles are very unobtrusive when worn on the belt of your pants, coat, or fanny pack.

IT'S IN THE BAG. . .

Like a builder, the muzzleloader shooter needs tools to maintain and load his rifle or shotgun at home and in the field. Bore preparation and ignition should be a given, not a concern, as the hunter settles his sights on game. To keep the bore clear from obstructions, moisture and fouling, a few ramrod attachments should be carried in your shooting bag. These include a bore brush, a threaded ball puller, a patch puller, and a fouling scraper for the breech. (If you have ever had wet powder caked in your breech you will know why a scraper is handy.) CVA's Muzzle Mitts are an excellent way to seal the business end of your muzzleloader from the elements. Electrician's tape also works well over the muzzle. A few large cleaning patches, like Ox-Yoke's 2-inch round, work great when used over a bore brush to keep your barrel clean and dry. Small containers of solvent, lubricant or rust inhibitor like Knight Oil or Natural Lube 1000 should accompany overnight hunters.

A pipe cleaner still works well to maintain clean, clear ignition ports in both percussion and flintlock guns.

FLINTLOCK IGNITION

Bag components for the flintlock should include flints, jaw leathers for gripping the flint, and a frizzen-cover, perhaps made from the finger of a leather glove, to help maintain a clean, dry striking surface and act as a safety device if the hammer should accidentally fall. Flinter's tools including vent pick, pan brush, flint hammer, and screw driver to tighten the jaws of the hammer are mandatory to help keep the pan clean, the vent hole open, and the flint sharp and adjusted correctly. Pan chargers with the all-important FFFFg priming powder can range from push-valved priming horns to small brass pan chargers. To maintain a dry pan charge, a water-resistant powder such as Mountain State Muzzleloading's Raincoat can be mixed with the powder without slowing ignition time. To keep the entire lock area protected from the elements, there is the Leather Pan Cover from October Country.

PERCUSSION IGNITION

Bag components for the percussion lock should include extra nipples and a nipple wrench. Nipple wrenches come in many styles from the very basic sliding T handle to the extra long for the modern in-lines that not only remove the nipple but the breech plug as well.

Cappers always come in handy, especially if you've ever tried placing a cap on a nipple when your fingers are frozen. Most cappers hold a good supply of #11 caps, musket caps, or 209 primers. Whether you're a traditionalist or a modernist, you have plenty to choose from, ranging from Tedd Cash's authentic 19th century replicas

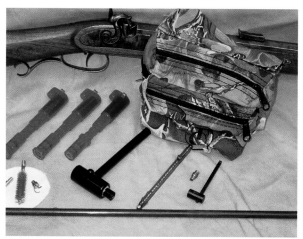

This compact hunting pouch contains speed loaders that hold powder and projectile, a short starter for introducing the projectile to the muzzle and starting it down the barrel, an in-line capper, a nipple wrench and a spare nipple, a Mountain State Muzzleloading Super Rod, a ball puller, bore brush, cleaning patch, and patch remover.

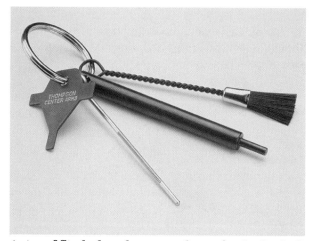

A ring of flintlock tools are mandatory for the flintlock hunter to keep the flash pan clean, the vent hole open, and the flint adjusted correctly.

A powder measure is the key to efficient loading and safe handling of muzzleloading propellants.

to Dixie Guns Works' brass in-line cappers to the new-age synthetic cappers including Knight's Fiber-Lite and Thompson/Center's U-View.

Other cap-related accessories are useful, too. A number of makers offers de-cappers to remove stubborn fired caps or snug-fitting caps from an unfired gun. To keep my #11 caps held in place and sealed from moisture I have long used Cap Guards from Ox-Yoke. They slip right over the cap and seal it directly to the nipple. There are also cap covers that slip right over the entire nipple and are held in place by the hammer.

SHORT STARTERS

These indispensable items are used to start the projectile down the bore, whether it be a patched round ball, lead slug, or a jacketed pistol bullet in a sabot. They are basically thick-handled tools with one or two "legs" or stubby ramrods that let you exert great pressure on the projectile as it enters the bore. Short starters range in style from antler-handled with a hickory long leg and a brass short leg to all wood to synthetic. I lost a short starter once in thick cover. Shortly thereafter I bought one with brass legs and an orange pool-ball palm saver. I've used it for years.

With the popularity of shooting lead slugs and sabot bullets, and the growing appreciation of the importance of a ramrod as a loading and cleaning tool, the T-handle short

starter gained popularity. Most manufacturers now offer T-handle starters that not only work as short starters, but also attach to the ramrod for better grip for loading and cleaning duties. Bullet companies such as Barnes, who offers the popular and great-performing Expander MZ all-copper bullet, offer an alignment tool to correctly load and seat their hollow point sabot bullets.

Some short starters double as self-contained powder and projectile loaders, too. Two of my favorites are the Ox-Yoke Cyclone Quick Loader and the RMC Magnum EC Loaders.

CHARGERS

The powder horn and flask have transported a lot of blackpowder over the years. Both are still made today and are very functional vessels. But remember, it doesn't matter if horns or flasks are spouted or not–do not use them to pour powder directly into your barrel! USE A POWDER MEASURE. Again, there are many shapes and style measures to choose from, ranging from traditional hollowed-out horn tips to the latest adjustable measures with spouts. You need a powder measure for loading from horn or flask in the field, and measuring your black powder or Pyrodex for your preloads at camp. T/C's U-View powder flask and measure eliminates the guesswork when measuring your hunting loads. The shotgun hunter will need a shot dipper to measure shot charges, and CVA

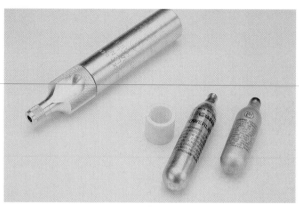

Have you ever forgot the powder before projectile, or in a location where discharging your muzzleloader is a problem? CO2 cartridge dischargers can get the job done safely.

ing Goex blackpowder and patched round ball, Pyrodex Select with a bore button and a lead slug, Pyrodex Pellets and a sabot bullet, or Elephant Brand blackpowder and bird shot: today's speed loaders handle them all. The shotgun hunter still needs a pocket for wads and over-shot cards. I have hunted extensively with Ox-Yoke Originals Speed Shells for rifle and shotgun as they facilitate fast reloading.

DISCHARGING

For the traveling hunter there are a few handy items to consider. When discharging your muzzleloader by firing it is not an option, you can use T/C's Magnum Silent Ball Discharger or Traditions' EZUnloader. These little guys use a blast of compressed carbon dioxide to blow the projectile free of the barrel without need of firing. Both are available with adapters to fit any muzzleloader.

Removable breech plugs in newer model flintlocks, many caplocks and all in-lines have made discharging loaded muzzleloaders a very simple task. Unscrewing the breech plug, pushing out the powder charge and projectile, and wiping the bore becomes an easy job. Not so with older fixed-breech guns!

and Traditions market volumetric measures that allow for equal measures of both powder and shot.

The ball bag and patched-ball loading block were, and are, commonly used to carry projectiles for rifles. The shot snake and shot pouch did the same for the scattergun. To traditional shooters, they still do. But in the hunting fields today, the preload is king. It doesn't matter if you're shoot-

4

Traditional Guns Shooting the Traditional Projectile

The percussion rifle cracked and the steel plate rang. A combination of excitement and fear had me gripping that 45-caliber longrifle with a 40-inch barrel as though I were holding on for dear life. The cloud of white smoke lifted and I saw the 18-inch square piece of 1/4-inch steel swinging on the chains that suspended it from a large maple tree. My friend, who had asked me over to try his father's muzzleloading rifle, asked, "What do you think?" I didn't know what to think. Like most Americans in the late 1960's, my only exposure to muzzleloader shooting had been watching Disney's Davy Crockett and prime time Daniel Boone. But after actually loading and firing a traditionally styled rifle, the loading and the visual and sound effects of ignition thrilled me to the bone.

The rifle I fired that day was a Dixie Gun Works Squirrel Rifle. Unbeknownst to me, I had started my muzzleloading career shooting a later version of the very first mass-produced muzzleloader, one that would kick off an entirely new era for muzzleloading in America.

'Way back in 1955 the late Turner Kirkland started Dixie Gun Works with a 12-page catalog and the Squirrel Rifle, the first production muzzleloader of this new age. A contemporary of Kirkland was Val Forgett. Forgett also had a fascination with America's original shooting irons. In 1957, he started Navy Arms Company, and it's not too surprising that Navy's first long gun offered was a modern copy of the 58-caliber Remington Zouave rifle. These two men took a dying pastime and the forgotten guns of our forefathers and gave them back to America.

Thirty years ago, around the time when I fired my first muzzleloading shot, Warren Center at Thompson/Center Arms had just finished designing an eye-catching, traditionally styled half-stock muzzleloader with the hunter in mind. The T/C Hawken was introduced in December

Traditionally-styled muzzleloaders are part of our American hunting heritage.

1970. The 28-inch barreled rifle was an instant success. Healthy whitetail populations, renewed hunter interest, and a movie called *Jeremiah Johnson*, with its wild-and-woolly-mountain-man hero, made the T/C Hawken a hit.

Connecticut Valley Arms entered the muzzleloading market in the early 1970s with kit guns that could be made at home. The CVA Mountain Rifle was a huge success. Lyman entered the market as well in the early '70's with its Great Plains Rifle, a faithful representation of the rifle carried across the Great Plains by pioneers and fur trappers.

Traditions entered the market in 1982 with a whole series of traditionally-styled, regional rifles such as the Pennsylvania, Kentucky, Shenandoah, and the Tennessee. Each of these aforementioned companies would go on to develop extensive lines of muzzleloading firearms and accessories.

Traditionally styled round ball rifles have a slow twist such as 1:60 or 1:66. That stubby little ball doesn't have to spin very fast to be accurate. However, it's a short-range

The same charge loaded in the same length barrel of same rifling and caliber will produce the same ballistics no matter what style the muzzleloader is. This hunter is holding Thompson/Center's Black Mountain Magnum Rifle.

The new generation of traditional style muzzleloaders are geared for both classic looks and hunting performance. From top to bottom: T/C's Black Mountain Magnum, Traditions' Hawken Woodsman, DGW's Jaeger Rifle, CVA's Mountain Rifle, Lyman's Great Plains Hunter, and Navy Arms' Pennsylvania Rifle.

True traditional replica rifles are handsome firearms. L to R: Austin & Halleck's Mountain Rifle, Tennessee Valley Muzzleloading's Virginia Rifle, and a custom Storey Side Hammer Rifle.

projectile, as it rapidly loses velocity and thus energy. Seeking good middle ground, Warren Center adopted a 1:48 twist in the T/C Hawken to stabilize both the patched round ball and the conical lead bullet, which maintains more knockdown energy over longer distance.

A NEW GENERATION OF TRADITIONALLY STYLED RIFLES

I personally hunt with all types of muzzleloading long arms, both percussion and flintlock. I hunt wild turkeys and upland game with shotguns and whitetail deer with traditionally styled rifles. But I also hunt the general firearms seasons for whitetails using a scoped modern in-line. In every marketplace there is an ebb and flow, and now it seems that interest in the traditionally-styled muzzleloader is on the rise again. The companies who made their mark offering traditionally styled muzzleloaders have never gone away. They now carry their original designs as well as modern but traditional-looking guns for a new century of primitive arms shooting.

Dixie Gun Works has the largest catalog of guns and accessories in the business. Their Early American Jaeger (German for "hunter") Rifle is a beautiful gun. This massive 54-caliber gun is offered in flint or percussion. It is handsomely and authentically designed with matte browned metal on an American Walnut full-length stock that features a sliding wooden patch box. The 27-5/8-inch barrel has a 1:24 inch twist. Dixie claimed the Jaeger would shoot round ball, slugs, and sabot bullets. We tested it at 50-yard targets. Eighty-five grains of FFg Goex blackpowder put five patched 230-grain Speer round balls into a 2-inch group. One hundred grains of Pyrodex Select put three 338-grain Buffalo Ballets into a 2-inch group. And 100 grains of Pyrodex Select put three 275-grain Barnes Expander MZ sabot bullets into a 1-inch group.

Navy Arms offers its Pennsylvania Long Rifle in flint or percussion. The sweeping, graceful lines of this style of rifle make it one of the most recognizable arms of American history. The full-stock 561/2-inch rifle features a 40-1/2-inch barrel with a 1:48 rate of twist. Seventy grains of FFFg Goex blackpowder moves a 45-caliber roundball along at over 1900 fps. Do not underestimate a well-placed .445-inch patched round ball. From squirrels to whitetails, this American original rifle and load would do Davy Crockett proud.

Thompson/Center Arms is keeping with their tradition of quality sidelock rifles with the Black Mountain Magnum (discontinued in 2004, alas). This sporterized, traditional muzzleloader features fiber optic sights and an elongated breech that allows for direct flame passage from the ignition to the barrel. The ignition source can be either a #11 percussion cap or the larger, hotter musket cap. The 26-inch barrel is rifled with a 1:28 twist and is heavy enough for 150-grain powder charges of either

FFG blackpowder, Pyrodex, or Pyrodex Pellets. The stock is available in either American walnut or black Rynite synthetic. This is a solid, well-balanced rifle that put three 295-grain CVA Power Belt bullets into a 1-½-inch group at 100 yards with a charge of 100 grains of FFg Goex blackpowder. This rifle, like the original T/C Hawken, was built with the hunter in mind.

Connecticut Valley Arms has brought back the gun that made the company famous: the 50-caliber Mountain Rifle. This workhorse is a representation of the no-frills rifle of the mountain man era and is designed for the round ball shooter with 1:66 rifling in a 32-inch barrel. The browned steel hardware on a maple stock is graced with a buckhorn rear sight and German silver wedge plates and blade front sight. Eighty grains of FFg Goex blackpowder push a 180-grain patched Speer round ball along at over 1600 fps.

Lyman muzzleloaders have great eye appeal. Its Great Plains Hunter is no exception. Offered in .50 or .54, flint or percussion, and in factory-assembled or kit form, this traditionally-styled rifle captures the look and feel of the frontier front-loader as few others do. Besides open sights, the Hunter has an optional rear peep and a front bead. Instead of a round ball twist, the Hunter has a 1:32 rifling rate. At the bench, 90 grains of Goex FFg produced 1- to 2-inch groups with both the 385-grain Great Plains Bullet and Lyman's 240-grain 45-caliber saboted bullet.

Traditions enters the new century with the 50- and 54-caliber Hawken Woodsman. A 28-inch barrel, adjustable sights, and a 1:48 twist allow the Woodsman to shoot balls, slugs and sabot bullets accurately. Other features include right or left hand models and a hunter-friendly oversized trigger guard for the crisp double set triggers. In 50-caliber, 90 grains of FFg pushing a .015 patched 177-grain round ball creates 1651 fps muzzle velocity and a muzzle energy of 1072 fpe. This rifle is a good choice for the close quarters woodland hunter.

Austin & Halleck's Mountain Rifle is a handsome half-stock with a 32-inch rust-browned barrel and lock and furniture set in curly maple. This rifle is offered with a

THE HEAD OF THE CLASS

A muzzleloading hunting rifle is a matter of personal preference as to design and function. Any one of the previously-mentioned guns just might catch your eye. Of these traditional offerings, I find the DGW Jaeger to be an excellent-shooting, authentically-designed rifle, at home in the woods or at a period re-enactment. For a sporterized hunting rifle, the no-frills T/C Black Mountain Magnum with fiber optic sights is an accurate, hard-hitting big game gun. But after handling the lot, what proved to be the head of the class for design, function, and accuracy in a truly classic rifle was the Lyman Great Plains Hunter.

If you have ever had the opportunity to hold an original early- to mid-1800s stout half-stock, you will appreciate that the 49-inch, 9-pound Great Plains Hunter is a very close replica. The traditionally shaped, nicely figured European walnut stock is made for fit and comfort with a 3-1/2-inch drop at heel and a 14-inch trigger pull. The 32-inch octagon barrel features a 1-in-32 twist with shallow .007 rifling with 5 lands and grooves for shooting lead slugs and sabot bullets. The barrel and furniture are deep blued, and the lock is case hardened with double set triggers. We replaced the front blade and buckhorn sights with Lyman's 57 GPR receiver peep sight and 37ML front sight. The rifle is pre-drilled to accept the 57 GPR. The 37ML white bead front sight that stands out in low light conditions is a modern version of William Lyman's original design. That design featured a light gathering vertical column of ivory set in the front sight, the forefather of the modern fiber optic sights.

My father and I further tested the 50-caliber percussion Great Plains Hunter. All shots were taken in groups of three at 50 yards. The first projectile out of the Great Plains Hunter was Lyman's own 335-grain lead Shocker sabot bullet. Ninety grains of Pyrodex RS created a tight 1-½-inch group. We found the Lyman sights very useful with their increased sight radius that allowed for precise aiming. Next we tried the PowerBelt Bullet with the same powder charge. This combination produced just under a 2-inch group. Knight's 310-grain lead sabot and T/C's 370-grain Maxi-Ball also produced a 2-inch group. D&D Bullets' new 300-grain CSP deer bullet over 90 grains of FFg Goex blackpowder produced a 3-inch cloverleaf.

Lyman's Great Plains hunter cannot be beat for traditional looks and performance.

1:66 twist round ball barrel or in a 1:28-twist conical/sabot barrel. Right out of the box the Mountain Rifle shot a 1-inch group with two of the shots touching. The 80-grain charge of Elephant FFg pushing a .010 Ox-Yoke Wonder Lubed patch cradling a .490 Buffalo swaged round ball produced 1666 feet per second velocity and 1091 foot pounds of energy. The Mountain Rifle comes standard with traditional buckhorn rear sight and silver blade front. The rifle will soon be available with adjustable fiber optic sights to appeal to a broader base of shooters.

LEST WE FORGET

The last half-century of muzzleloading in America has seen traditional styling and performance progress to those that push the envelope of modern technology. The new rifles from the manufacturers of traditional and classic styles are a pleasant blend of yesterday and today. They are user-friendly, geared for accuracy, hard hitting and pleasing to the eye. If you are looking for a new muzzleloader for big game, don't forget the original muzzleloading companies that continue to work at putting history in our hands.

LEAD:MUZZLELOADING'S TRADITIONAL PROJECTILE

When I was growing up, one of the many hunting books in our home was a 1960 collection of stories compiled by Raymond R. Camp titled *Hunting Trails*. The basis for a story of his, "The Magic Rifle," was the traditional beef shoots held each spring in Cataloochie, North Carolina. The description of one competitor, "old Dan," and his attention to the process of loading captured my imagination. "First he swabbed the barrel. Then the powder was measured carefully in a hollowed boar's tooth and slowly poured down the barrel. His companion nodded approvingly as he slapped the stock to settled the grains. The carefully molded bullet was then shrouded in a square of oiled linen and seated in the muzzle with a sharp rap of the hickory starter. Trimming the patch with a razor-sharp knife, old Dan then thrust the bullet home with an even sweep of the ramrod. Then, with a thin priming wire he picked at the hole and channel, measured a pinch of fine priming powder into the pan and snapped the cover down."

ORIGINS OF LEAD

Not only did the fictional old Dan load the muzzleloader a step at a time and win the beef shoot, he molded the bullets, too! Running ball, as it is called, was not a novelty for old Dan. It was a necessity. Like his forefathers, old Dan molded his own bullets because store-bought bullets weren't readily available, and for people of meager means it was the only way to get them. As the pioneers and mountain men had discovered, lead is readily available, occurring most commonly in the sulfide mineral

Galena, a soft, heavy, malleable, dull gray metallic element, would be forever tied to muzzleloading in America.

galena. Mountain men often referred to the substance of their projectiles as galena.

Not a rare mineral by any means, galena is a heavy, gray mineral with a metallic luster. Galena, basically lead ore, is a sulfur compound of lead. In its purest state it consists of 86.6 per cent lead and 13.4 per cent sulfur by weight. Galena is found in the form of masses in limestone or as fragments in rocks and soil. When melted and purified, galena becomes the lead that muzzleloader hunters know and love so well.

Besides being so common, lead melts at a mere 621 degrees Fahrenheit, so a wood stove or campfire is more than hot enough to run ball. Cheap, easily available, reuseable–it's no wonder that lead was destined to be the projectile of America's muzzleloaders.

WHY LEAD?

Every muzzleloader shooter should cast lead projectiles at least once, if for no other reason than the sake of the knowledge, historical appreciation, and effort involved. I was brought up in a household where bullet casting was a normal activity. My older brother was a skilled bullet caster as he made pistol bullets for his .357 and .44 magnum revolvers. We didn't use a small, electric lead furnace. We used a plumber's cast iron lead kettle that held about a half-gallon of molten lead heated by a 20-lb. propane tank. We didn't run ball often, but when we did, we ran a lot using scrap plumbing lead lines.

Our father always insisted we cast in a well-ventilated area, wearing leather work shoes, long pants, long sleeve jackets, goggles, and gauntlet. On one of the luckiest days of my life I knocked a full kettle of molten lead onto our concrete garage floor. Because of our dress, we were unscathed. When my big brother got done lumping me, we both noticed an amazing, continuous sheet of lead across the floor. Due to the properties of lead, we were able to fold up the sheet of soft, pliable metal and put it

Accuracy is no stranger to the patched round ball as demonstrated by this 50-caliber DGW Tennessee Mountain Rifle with interchangeable locks.

Soft lead flattens quickly and transfers energy effectively. Both of these round balls were retrieved from whitetail deer.

back in the melting pot, skimming off the crud and casting bullets again.

Besides its availability and ease of handling, the density of lead makes it an excellent projectile. Its very mass makes it retain velocity and energy as no other practical metal can. These properties become evident as you cast, load, and shoot lead bullets out of muzzleloading firearms. Lead is the best medium, period. It is dense; it melts, molds, and conforms easily; and it remains intact on impact. Casting your own bullets is similar to fletching your own arrows: it puts you in touch with the primitive roots of your passion.

A ROUND BALL EDUCATION

Casting round balls for my first muzzleloading rifle in 1975 made me understand the relationship between the undersized .440 ball, a lubricated patch, and the rifling in the barrel. I shot sprued and swaged round balls at everything from targets to squirrels and whitetails with that little half-stock using 70 grains of FFg blackpowder. (A sprued ball is one cast in a mold. The "sprue" is a small, raised circle of lead left on the ball by the mold channel. A "swaged" ball is formed under pressure in a die.)

The whole concept of the ball being cradled in a patch and guided over rifling it never even touches fueled my fire for this primitive pursuit. But it wasn't until I began retrieving spent projectiles while skinning game and rendering venison that I saw lead's ability to deform yet stay intact. The trait of this small projectile to expand on impact made for excellent knockdown power on deer sized game. I became so confident with the 45-caliber rifle that I took it caribou hunting in 1981. I did kill a bull caribou. But I also realized afterward that I had hunted big game with a pea-shooter.

My next round ball rifle experience involved a 50-caliber double rifle. It was successful on close range whitetails, but on a Wyoming pronghorn hunt in 1983 its curved, loopy trajectory took over. Nevertheless I successfully lobbed one in there at more than 100 yards and proudly took a nice antelope with a .490 patched round ball. Both of these rifles possessed a 1:48 twist. I could shoot good targets, but consistency was lacking. By the mid-1980s I was shooting a 54-caliber round ball rifle

Hunting guns designed to shoot lead conical bullets deliver the downrange energy needed for big game. The sustained energy of this T/C Maxi-Ball fired from the author's custom 54-caliber rifle flipped a bull elk off its feet.

with deep .012" rifling with a 1:60 twist. Discovering the benefits of the slower twist's effects on a patched ball was enlightening. I shot my first cloverleaf the first trip to the shooting range. A .535, 230-grain patched ball pushed by a 90-gr. charge of FFg produced 1235 fpe moving at 1555 fps. This has been a very effective hunting caliber for big game. But even this round ball fades to 513 ft lbs of energy at 100 yards.

As I have learned at the range and in the field, in 32- to 62-caliber flintlock and percussion rifles, the patched round ball is a sub-100-yard shooter as loss of energy and higher trajectory diminish its effectiveness. But within these parameters, a round ball rifle can be a tack driver. A DGW Tennessee Mountain Rifle of ours with a 1:56 twist shoots 1-inch clusters on demand.

SLUG POWER

One evening in 1988, I received a call from my local taxidermist. He had been caping out a nice 6x6 bull elk. He called me after discovering a round ball in the bull's neck area. The elk had been killed by a center-fire rifle hunter, but someone, once upon a time, had plunked a round ball into the animal. The round ball had obviously been used beyond its effective limits as it was hardly damaged where it rested under the hide.

I had drawn an elk tag that year and was determined to have better results than the hapless round ball hunter who wounded that bull. In those days, I had not done much conical shooting. But that was about to change. Conicals are much more massive than roundballs in the same bore size, and more moving mass increases down-

These lead projectiles include (l to r) Dixie Gun Works Cast Minie Bullet, Mushroom Express Bullet, Thompson Center's Maxi-Ball (lubed), CVA Deerslayer, Buffalo Bullet's Ball-et, Lee's REAL (Rifle Engraved At Loading) Bullet, Buffalo Bullet's Swaged Round Ball, and a round ball home-cast with a LEE bullet mold (note sprue).

Shotgun pattern density and downrange energy are determined by barrel choke, shot size and powder charge.

The bases of these bullets are designed to obdurate, or expand on ignition, to engage the rifling in the barrel.

range power. Unlike the patched sphere that prefers deep rifling and a slow rate of twist, the elongated lead slug usually likes shallow .005 rifling and faster twists ranging from 1:20 to 1:32. This is because the increased length of the conical bullet requires more spin to stabilize it. When backed by stout powder charges, lubricated, elongated lead conical bullets possess unrivaled knockdown power.

After testing several brands of conicals, I selected Thompson/Center's original Maxi-Ball. The Maxi-Ball design relies on oversized bearing bands to gain purchase on the barrel rifling as you load the slug. Upon ignition, the solid base of the Maxi-Ball expands to seal the gases and further engage the rifling. Unlike the other bullet designs tested for the elk hunt, the T/C slug design worked unbelievably well in my 54-caliber, 1:60 round ball gun. The combination of a 100-gr. charge of FFg behind a Wonder Wad and a 430-gr. Maxi-Ball has taken considerable game, the most notable being a large Missouri whitetail buck and two Colorado bull elk that were knocked right off their feet. Then again, 1869 fpe of muzzle energy should! This slug still packed 1278 fpe at 100 yards. That's more energy than the .54 round ball delivered at the muzzle!

During the last 20 years I have had the opportunity to shoot a variety of lead conicals with a variety of fast-twist muzzleloading rifles of traditional and modern designs. The Hornady Great Plains Bullet, Lee's REAL Bullet (Rifling Engraved At Loading), and Buffalo Bullet Company's Maxi-Hunter have performed well on deer-sized game and can handle larger species without breaking a sweat. Some conicals feature hollow points for enhanced expansion while others incorporate a hollow base design that expands, or obdurates, during ignition to engage the rifling. Two saboted lead bullets that have performed very well for me have been Knight's 310-grain and Lyman's 335-gr. Shocker.

If you are looking for a lead slug shooter of traditional design, Lyman's 50-caliber, 1:32 Great Plains Hunter can't be beat for looks and performance. The targets that this gun produced rival any modern day muzzleloader, in-line or back-hammer. But even with an exceptionally accurate rifle such as the Lyman, the trajectory and dwindling energy of the conical slug make it suitable for distances no greater than 150 yards.

THE LEAD PELLET

From single-shot full-choke turkey guns to 20 and 12 gauge doubles, to a 62-cal./20-ga. flintlock fowler, our family has always enjoyed muzzleloading shotguns. And although other alternatives are available, our projectile of choice is the lead pellet. Why? Because like the round ball and slug, the soft lead pellet flattens quickly and transfers energy effectively to the game. Lead shot patterns well and carries well, too.

Volume-for-volume loading (equal volumes of both powder and shot) has long been the rule of thumb to begin load patterning with muzzleloading shotguns. Seventy grains of blackpowder is the volumetric equivalent of one ounce of shot. With modern gun manuals and load experimentation, you can create lethal shot patterns for small game, wild turkeys and waterfowl. Larger pellets sustain more energy than the smaller pellets when it comes to shotgun loads. That is why #4 or #5 pellets are harder-hitting turkey loads as opposed to #6 or #7-1/2 for upland game. Chokes, wads and shot cups control the pellets in a shotgun barrel. Most turkey and waterfowl hunters shoot full choke for the tightest possible pattern and longest range. Depending on the upland game hunted, hunters can chose from the tighter modified choke, to the wide-open cylinder bore. Shotgun patterning is the equivalent of sighting-in a rifle. A good shot pattern has few gaps and features an even dispersion of the pellets.

Non-toxic shot regulations and barrels to handle non-toxic shot have been an issue for several years. First there was steel shot, then bismuth, and Federal's tungsten/iron and tungsten/polymer blends. All of these lead substitutes are less dense than lead to one degree or another, and their performance has never quite equaled that of lead. Now, however, we have a new shot pellet that rivals lead in performance: Hevi-Shot. Lead weighs in at 11.1 gr/cc. Hevi-Shot weighs in at 12.0 gr/cc. This past turkey season I put the non-toxic Hevi-Shot through patterning and hunting tests. It felt like lead, it patterned great on a turkey target, and it flattened a 20-lb. gobbler. Remington recently added Environ-Metal, the originator of Hevi-Shot, to their lineup. I believe we will be seeing more of this non-toxic substitute in the future in both pellet and bullet form.

5

Modern Muzzleloaders Shooting Modern Projectiles

odern muzzleloading rifles have the look and feel of a centerfire rifle. Gun designs have come a long way in providing accuracy and acceptably flat hunting trajectories by matching bullets, powder charges and barrel twists for optimum performance. Many muzzleloader hunters today apparently aren't concerned with nostalgia. They're concerned with efficiency, accuracy, convenience and performance. Even Traditions' PA Pellet flintlock and the Thompson/Center Firestorm flintlock have removable breech plugs, synthetic stocks and fiber optic sights. Modern muzzleloading rifles feature adjustable triggers and sights; synthetic, wood and laminated stocks; and 209 shotgun primer ignition. This new breed of front-stuffers features straight pull plungers; bolt-action, break-action, and pivoting breech blocks that facilitate easy loading and easy cleaning; removable breech plugs; and precision barrels that are scope-ready and have bullet-aligning muzzles.

The results are in. Consumer interest and sales speak for themselves. Muzzleloader hunting with modern rifles geared toward the big game hunter is at an all-time high.

Modern muzzleloaders such as this Knight Rifle are the favored gun of many big game hunters today.

KNIGHT RIFLES

Tony Knight raised the bar on muzzleloading performance in 1985 with the introduction of his modern muzzleloading rifle, the MK-85. The MK-85 featured an in-line plunger-style ignition, a 1:28 barrel twist to handle modern projectiles such as the saboted pistol bullet, and a double safety system. My father and I have taken a fair amount of game with our 50-caliber MK-85 Knight Hawk with a thumbhole stock shooting 100-grain Hodgdon charges behind 250-grain Barnes MZ all-copper bullets. The most notable of these were two Iowa bucks taken on the same day with the same gun, my dad's buck in

the morning and my buck (pictured on the cover) in the evening.

Tony Knight again raised the bar with his bolt-action Disc Rifle in 1997. "Precise" is perhaps the best way to describe the design and performance of the Knight D.I.S.C. rifle (Disc Ignition System Concept). This 43-inch, 8-lb. 50-caliber offering features a 24-inch barrel with a 1:28 barrel twist designed to push saboted bullets with stiff charges–"stiff" meaning 100-grain loads of FFg blackpowder or Pyrodex or three 50-grain Pyrodex Pellets. The composite Monte Carlo stock is available in

The newest generation of modern muzzleloading rifles comes in a variety of actions and configurations including (top to bottom) the break-open action of the Thompson/Center Encore 209x50 with walnut fore end and butt stock; the pivoting breech of the synthetic stocked T/C Omega; and the camouflage and bolt action of the Winchester X-150.

black or camouflage finish. Other features include blued or stainless Green Mountain barrels, adjustable Timney triggers, removable stainless steel breech plugs, drilled and tapped receivers, the Knight patented double safety system, fully adjustable rear sights, rubber recoil pads, and instructional videos.

At the heart of the Disc Rifle is a bolt-action ignition system that uses unique plastic ignition discs carrying a #11 percussion cap or the hotter 209-shotshell primer. The action of lifting the bolt and sliding it to the rear of the action exposes a priming port where the disc with the primer is placed. The motion of sliding the bolt forward and down mates the disc with the breech plug and provides a weatherproof ignition system. The 209 primers are easily finger pressed into the disc before it's placed into the priming chamber. The 209-shotshell primer promotes hotter and more positive ignition, but it's also necessary to burn the heavy powder charges for which the gun was designed. For example, a #11 percussion cap in a 45-caliber DISC rifle shooting a 150-grain sabot bullet pushed by a 100-grain charge of FFg blackpowder or Pyrodex produces 1767 fps velocity at the muzzle. The same load pushed by two 50-grain Pyrodex Pellets and a 209 primer produces 1850 fps muzzle velocity. The 209 primer accounts for the difference in velocity.

The 50-caliber DISC rifle my father and I put through its paces featured a black composite stock and blued hardware. Our bullet selection was simple: Barnes Red Hot bullets with sabots. These all-copper bullets have performed accurately with flawless downrange performance on a variety of game. The propellant of choice was Pyrodex Pellets. With varmints in mind we topped the rifle off with a 4-12 power Bushnell Elite 3200 riflescope that features a 40mm objective front lens for excellent light gathering abilities, a 3-inch eye relief, and 1/4 inch click value at 100 yards for easy sight adjustment. We also employed a Bushnell Yardage Pro Compact 600 laser rangefinder to ensure shooting within the rifle's limits.

Our proven big game hunting load has long been two 50-grain pellets pushing a Barnes 250-grain all-copper Red Hot sabot bullet at almost 1700 fps with 1580 ft. lbs. of energy. With not quite 6 inches of drop at 150 yards, this is an excellent big game load. But woodchuck accuracy cannot tolerate 6 inches of drop. To solve this, we opted for the 180-gr. Barnes with three 50-grain pellets at 2277 fps. The 8-lb. DISC rifle comfortably handled the stiff charge as we sighted in the rifle. Shooting for groups initially, the rifle and load produced a 4-shot cloverleaf, before sighting in, right on at 100 yards. The flatter trajectory of this all-copper bullet would eventually print half an inch high at 50 yards and a pleasing 2.85 inches low at 150 yards.

Knight also offers the DISC rifle in 45-caliber. For those who wonder if a .45 can deliver the goods, I have news for you. Three 50-grain Pyrodex Pellets pushed

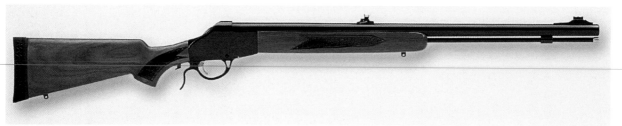

The Knight Revolution comes with a 2 1/2-inch, three shot group at 100-yards guarantee.

a 125-grain bullet out the spout at more than 2500 fps. That's about 72% faster than a hot .357 Magnum equivalent load. Barnes Red Hot bullets are also available in 150- and 180-grain weights in 45 caliber. All three bullets have a downrange drop within an inch of each other out to 200 yards. It is just a matter of finding which load works best in your rifle.

As the cream of the crop, Knight offers the Master Hunter DISC rifle. This 50-cal. honey features gold plated trigger and triggerguard, a jeweled bolt, and a tooled laminated stock with thumbhole grip and Monte Carlo cheek piece.

The smartly-designed T/C Omega is an excellent modern muzzleloading rifle.

Many hunters find that the DISC rifles often perform best with loose Pyrodex and blackpowder charges. To capitalize on this, Knight introduced the 52-caliber Disc Extreme rifle. It's designed to shoot a heavy 375-grain bullet at high velocity and incorporates Knight's innovative Powerstem breechplug to enhance powder charge combustion in the barrel.

The Knight Revolution is the latest introduction from this creative muzzleloading pioneer. If you think that all of the new breed of muzzleloaders look alike, think again. No plunger or bolt here. The Revolution has the look and feel of a sporterized Winchester Model 1885 High Wall cartridge rifle. A pivoting breechblock is the most notable feature of this new 50-caliber muzzleloader. Jacking the trigger guard forward allows you to cock the hammer and open the primer chamber. Knight's full plastic jacket DISC 209 primer slips into the breechplug. Pull the trigger guard back in place and you're locked and ready. Easy, straight-through cleaning is made possible by the rifle's Quick Detachable Action. Its precision Green Mountain rifle barrel with a 1:28 twist comes with a guarantee of 2 ½-inch, three-shot groups at 100 yards. The Knight Revolution is available in blued or stainless, with black or camouflage synthetic, walnut, or laminated stocks.

THOMPSON/CENTER ARMS

The T/C Encore 209X50 magnum muzzleloader was introduced in the late 1990s. Its simple break action, when closed, seals in the 209-shotshell primer for waterproof hunting. The removable breech plug with the EZ Tip extractor makes cleaning and removing unfired charges a snap. With its exposed hammer and patented hammerblock safety, the Encore is a very safe rifle that is easy to prime and shoot. When used with the Shock Wave bullet, co-developed with Hornady Manufacturing, you've got a hard-hitting hunting bullet and an easy-handling rifle. Although the Encore is capable of handling 150-grain charges, the one Dad and I tested preferred two 50-grain Triple Seven Pellets and a 295-gr. PowerBelt bullet. A variant of the Encore, the new Katahdin carbine with 20-inch ported barrel makes a mighty convenient hunting partner.

In early 2003 I received an initial run 45-caliber Omega Rifle. Oh boy, I thought, another blue barreled, black synthetic stocked muzzleloader! Whoopee. But it

The T/C Encore 209x50 is a very handy rifle that is easy to prime, shoot and clean.

didn't take long to realize that this rifle exhibited a whole new concept of the in-line muzzleloader and a totally new design of breech that simply swings down and away exposing the in-line breech plug for a) installation of a 209 shotgun primer and b) easy removal of the breech plug for uninhibited, straight-through barrel cleaning. And although modern in concept, the Omega rifle is a back-hammer percussion gun.

T/C rifles have always possessed the feel of a north-woods deer gun. The Omega is no exception at 42 inches long and 7 lbs. weight. The 1:28 twist, 28-inch in-line ignition barrel pretty much dictates pelletized powder and conical bullets. Although quality Tru-Glo fiber optic sights come standard on the barrel, my father and I opted to try the new Bushnell Elite 3200 Fire-Fly scope on the Omega as the stock comb is elevated for scope use. We decided to shake out the outfit with Aero-Tip 225-grain PowerBelt bullets and Hodgdon's new 45-caliber Triple Seven pellets.

The Omega is rated for 150-grain powder charges of blackpowder or Pyrodex. Triple Seven produces 20% more energy than standard Pyrodex, so we took a walk on the safe side and loaded only two 50-grain pellets in the Omega. The first sighting-in shooting session of 20 shots concluded with a three-shot 1-inch group. Removing the Gorilla-Greased breech plug was extremely easy. The sulfur-free Triple Seven along with the simple swinging

breech make the Omega the quickest-cleaning muzzle-loading rifle that you will find. On the next trip to the shooting range my father produced a three-shot, 1 1/2-inch group at 100 yards. The two-pellet, 100-grain charge of Triple Seven behind the 225-grain .45 bullet produced over 1700 fps muzzle velocity with almost 1450 fpe. But how would the Omega perform on deer? We were eager to find out.

On two occasions last October I had observed both bucks and does enter the corner of a woodland opening at sunset. I thought this would be an excellent opportunity for my father. The field's open ground had a roll in it, so the hunter would have to have some elevation to see over the rise. By using one section of a ladder stand I could get my father eight feet off the ground.

On Halloween eve I tucked dad and the .45 Omega into the tree line opposite the trail entrance at 3:00 p.m. As the sun's disc prepared to do its daily disappearing act, a lone deer appeared at the far corner trail entrance 125 yards away. The Bushnell Elite 3200 scope gathered the fading light as my father settled the crosshairs on the moving buck at 100 yards. I heard the report of the Omega and headed down the trail with great expectations. From the edge of the opening I could see a large cloud of Triple Seven vapor as it hung in the evening air. The expression on my dad's face indicated that the .45 Omega is indeed a deer gun. In spades.

The Remington 700ML blackpowder muzzleloader is modeled after the famous Model 700 bolt-action. It shoots like one, too!

REMINGTON

Throughout its 180-plus-year history, the Remington Arms Company has always produced appealing and dependable firearm designs. It's often ironic how things tend to go full circle. Eliphalet Remington started making 50-caliber flintlock rifles in 1816. In 1996, the company he founded introduced a muzzleloader that responded to the needs of a new generation. Based on the tried and true Model 700 bolt action, the 700 ML features a 24-inch barrel on a 44-inch rifle that weighs in at 7-¾ lbs. The 700 ML shoulders like an old friend with its ½-inch drop at the comb, 3/8-inch drop at the heel, and a 13-3/8-inch length of pull. Except for the visible ramrod, the Model 700 in-line black powder rifle looks and feels like a standard centerfire Model 700 short action. The 700 ML is offered in blued carbon steel, while the stainless version is the 700 MLS. Both are cradled by a synthetic stock remarkably like that of the 700 centerfires.

Unlike the *klatch-poof-boom* of the lock of the first Remington flinter in 1816, the new 700 ML features a completely modern in-line striker design with a lock time of 3.0 milliseconds. Instead of pulling the hammer back to cock this muzzleloader, you simply work the bolt action to cock the firing pin. The open breech design features a stainless steel breech plug that can accept a #11 percussion cap, a musket cap, or a 209-primer. The safety is within easy thumb reach at the rear of the bolt. Remington chose a 1:28 rifling twist for its new black powder rifles to take full advantage of today's enormous selection of conicals

and saboted bullets. Right out of the box this muzzleloader had the balance and feel of a quality gun. Open sights consisted of a ramp bead front and adjustable rear, but the receiver was drilled and tapped for Remington 700 short action scope bases. So without hesitation we mounted a Simmons Diamond Mag riflescope on the 700 ML. It featured variable magnification of 3.8-12 x 44 wide angle with Simmons' Smart Reticle, which allows the shooter to acquire the target quickly and accurately.

It was a clear April morning when my father and I swabbed the bore, snapped some caps, and prepared to wring out the 700 ML on the bench. The manufacturer's recommended charge was 100 grains FFg, so we used two 50-grain Pyrodex pellets. Above the pellets we used Thompson/Center's Bore Buttons to stabilize the load, as it has proven to create tighter groups. Following the initial sighting-in, the T/C's 370-gr. Maxi-Ball shot a three-shot, 3-inch group at 100 yards. That would make a fine deer-hunting load. Next we tried Remington's Copper Solid 289-gr. all-copper bullet with the same two-pellet load. You could say this sabot bullet was designed for this gun. The results were a 1-inch group. Four days later my father tried it again to see if this gun, load, and bullet, were really this accurate. This time he shot a 1-inch group. (Without T/C Bore Buttons our groups increased in excess of 2 inches.) At 100 yards, this bullet was traveling at 1270 fps and sustaining 1034 ft. lbs. of energy. Zeroed in at 100 yards, the bullet had a trajectory 1.6 inches high at 50 yards and 7.5 inches low at 150 yards. These results weren't merely acceptable–they were super!

The Austin & Halleck 420 series are handsome and accurate rifles.

WINCHESTER

The 45-caliber Winchester X-150 muzzleloader we tested featured a blued barrel with a stainless steel bolt action and breech. A 26-inch fluted barrel with a 1:28 rifling twist and a well-designed composite stock complete the package. At 8 lbs. and 45 inches long, this rifle is well balanced. Like many modern in-lines, the X-150 features 209 ignition, fiber optic sights, and a removable breech plug. The fiber optic sights seemed a tad too small, so my father mounted a T/C Hawken Hunter 4x32 Center Plex Reticle scope on the rifle. Then we gathered powder and projectiles and headed for the shooting range.

By the time hunting season rolled around, and after extensive testing, our load of choice turned out to be two 50-gr. Pyrodex Pellets pushing a 225-gr. PowerBelt Aero Tip bullet at 1968 fps with 1935 fpe. PowerBelt Bullets, a BPI product, have come on as solid performers in recent years. They load easily and shoot great. The Winchester muzzleloader with this load proved to be a nice shooting, comfortable rifle, with a smooth-working bolt and quick, reliable ignition. My father dropped a whitetail with this setup at 60 yards. Despite having a proven winner in the X-150, Winchester isn't standing still: the company's new Winchester Apex Magnum 209 features a swing-action design on a 44-inch 81/4-lb. rifle in 45 or 50 caliber that is meant to give the T/C Omega a run for its money.

AUSTIN & HALLECK

The Austin & Halleck 420 series bolt-action muzzleloading rifles are probably the handsomest, best-finished guns on the market. They feature octagon-to-straight barrels and nicely figured wood stocks with classic 20 lpi checkering. A large receiver makes seating a 209 primer quick as a flash, and fully adjustable triggers facilitate comfortable and accurate shooting with 150-gr. charges in the 1:28 twist 26-in. barrel. When used in the 420, Hodgdon's Triple Seven and Barnes bullets are capable of consistent 1-inch groups at 100 yards. For the discriminating muzzleloader shooter and hunter, these rifles are the last word in tasteful inlines.

SAVAGE'S 10ML-II

Savage Arms set the world of muzzleloading a-buzz in 2000 when the venerable company announced the first smokeless powder–that's right, I said smokeless powder–muzzleloader, the Savage 10ML-II. This 50-caliber, bolt-action, 209-primed, high-performance muzzleloader features a removable breech plug with vent liner, a receiver drilled and tapped for scope installation, and fiber optic sights. But its ability to handle non-corrosive smokeless powder sets it apart. Because the rifle is built to handle the pressures of smokeless powder (producing over 2300 fps velocity and 3000 fpe), blackpowder, Pyrodex, and other replica powders can be used as well. DO NOT use smokeless powder in ANY other muzzleloading firearm unless expressly recommended for such by the manufacturer. Let me repeat that. As of this writing, the Savage 10ML-II is the ONLY muzzleloader capable of handling smokeless powder. The Savage 10ML-II has proven itself as a well-constructed and very accurate muzzleloading firearm featuring a unique ignition module that is seated into chamber of the rifle like a cartridge. Top whitetail photographer and writer Charlie Alsheimer swears by his Savage smokeless muzzleloader.

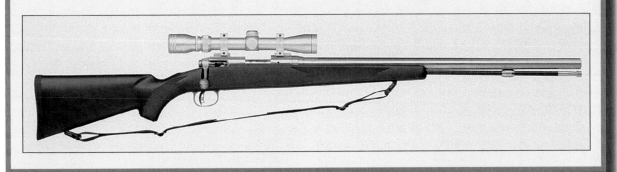

Goex blackpowder works wonderfully in modern muzzleloaders. But the top choice of modern muzzleloader shooters is the replica powders and pellets produced by Hodgdon (Pyrodex and Triple Seven).

SHOOTING MODERN PROJECTILES

Modern muzzleloaders feature super-short lock times, hot ignition, and quality barrels with fast rates of twist suited for shooting elongated, conical bullets. Which conical is the one for your rifle? Testing at the rifle range is the only way to find out. Downrange performance is the key to successful shooting. Yes, accuracy is essential. But trajectory and the ballistics of velocity in feet per second (fps) and energy in foot-pounds (fpe) are what separate great big game bullets from the also-rans.

So what bullet will it be? Buffalo Bullets SSB (Super Saboted Bullet), Hornady's SST polymer tip bullet, T/C's Shockwave bullet, or the PowerBelt from Blackpowder Products, Inc., all of them excellent bullets, represent only the tip of the iceberg as far as bullet selection is concerned.

The fast twists found in modern in-line rifles, the most popular being the 1:28, are made for shooting the modern conical projectile. Why? Two reasons: energy and sectional density.

Although accurate, the round ball loses energy rapidly because its mass is restricted by its diameter. The less mass the projectile has, the less energy it can retain. Conicals, being longer than they are wide, have greater mass than roundballs and can therefore retain more energy. And retained energy is what puts down the animal.

This retained energy comes at a price, however, and this is where sectional density comes in. Sectional density, the measurement of a projectile's mass in relationship to its diameter or length, determines how fast the bullet must spin in order to remain stable in flight. The higher the sectional density, the faster the rate of twist must be and vice versa. For example, the patched round ball has a low sectional density and performs best with a slow rate of twist. Being longer, conicals require a faster twist to stabilize their greater mass. This is why slow-twist 1:60 and 1:66 barrels are often referred to as "roundball barrels" and 1:24 to 1:48 barrels are considered conical barrels.

The introduction of plastic sabots in the 1980's by Del Ramsey and his Muzzleload Magnum Products (MMP) coincided nicely with Tony Knight's introduction of the modern muzzleloader in 1985. The sabot is analogous to the patch on a roundball: whereas the cloth patch grips the rifling for the round ball and seals the gases of ignition, the cup base of the plastic sabot expands to seal the gases and engage the rifling with the sabot sleeves that cradle the conical bullet. Both the cloth patch and sabot drop off once the projectile exits the barrel. A 50-caliber rifle shooting a 45-caliber saboted bullet achieves superior trajectory and ballistics when compared to a 50-caliber rifle shooting a 50-cal. (.495) patched roundball. A recent variant of the sabot, the PowerBelt bullet from Blackpowder Products, Inc., incorporates a snap-on skirt rather than a plastic jacket to engage the rifling and seal the gases. The PowerBelt bullet is very popular for its ability to load easily and shoot accurately.

In recent years the 150-grain powder charge has become the big thing. It's generally accepted as the stiffest blackpowder or replica blackpowder charge that can be safely used in guns rated for it. It's definitely not for older muzzleloaders. If your hunting situation dictates shooting

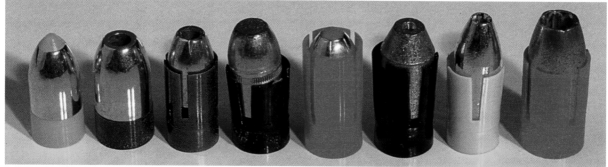

Plastic skirts and sabots allow each one of these modern projectiles to perform in modern muzzleloading rifles. L to R: PowerBelt Arrow-Tip, PowerBelt Hollow-Point, T/C XTP Magnum Bullet, 300 gr. Speer jacketed pistol bullet, T/C Power Tip Express, Knight 310 gr. lead, Barnes 45-cal Expander MZ, and the Barnes workhorse 250-gr. Expander MZ.

Three consistent performers used by the author and his father in a variety of modern rifles include the easy-loading PowerBelt bullet, the Knight 310-gr. lead bullet, and the 250-gr. Barnes Expander MZ.

If you are thinking big game, the Barnes all-copper muzzleloading projectiles such as this 245-gr. Spit-Fire perform great, as they consistently produce the entrance and exit holes desired from a hunting bullet.

at longer ranges, then you'll see the benefits in trajectory and downrange energy of using this magnum powder charge. For example, a 45-caliber 195-gr. PowerBelt bullet fired with two 50-gr. Pyrodex Pellets from a rifle zeroed at 150 yards will drop 15.4 inches at 250 yards. The same bullet fired at the same range with three 50-gr. Pyrodex Pellets hits 8.9 inches low. The 100-grain load has more than 1000 fpe at 150 yards while the 150-grain load still possesses almost 1000 fpe at 250 yards. Why is this important? Bullet performance on impact, that's why. A copper-jacketed lead pistol bullet or an all-copper bullet can neither expand

nor mushroom in the absence of enough energy to do so. MMP now offers the new Ballistic Bridge Sub Base to handle the heat and protect the sabot from the stiff charges of blackpowder and Hodgdon super-size loads.

Long-range shooting is nothing to guess at. Shooting data offered by powder and bullet companies should be adhered to. (The Barnes Ballistics Program is an excellent computational tool for the long-range shooter.) Comfort, accuracy, and your potential shooting distance should always dictate your choice of projectile and powder charge for your modern muzzleloading rifle.

LONG-RANGE ELK

Randy Brooks took this magnificent elk in December 2003 with a Knight Disc Extreme muzzleloader firing the new long-range 245-gr. 50-caliber Barnes Spit-Fire MZ bullet. Hunting in New Mexico with Ross Johnson Outfitters, Randy killed the bull, which scored 394-6/8, at 340 yards. Several factors contributed to this successful extreme-range shooting. First, both rifle and bullet were capable of excellent accuracy. A load of three 50-gr. Pyrodex pellets behind the 245-grain spitzer-shaped bullet produced a muzzle velocity of 2200 fps. Knowing he'd likely be shooting at long distance, Randy sighted in the scoped rifle to place the Spit-Fire bullet 6 inches high at 100 yards, providing a dead-on zero of 240 yards. Randy ran this load through the Barnes Ballistics program. The resulting trajectory printout was taped upside-down to the rifle's stock, allowing him to check bullet drop by simply tilting the rifle to the left.

Randy and his guide had spotted the elk as it bedded down and were reasonably sure the bull was still in the area. Once he found a suitable shooting site, Randy took time to draw a map of the area, using a laser rangefinder to pre-determine the distances to several different checkpoints (a tree,

shed antlers, etc.). That told him exactly how much holdover to use at those reference points. Finally, Randy placed his backpack over a boulder, giving him a solid, sandbag-like rest. Many years of hunting experience had Randy expecting the bull to leave his bed somewhere around 1:00 p.m. The bull lurched to his feet just 10 minutes ahead of schedule. Taking the 45-degree slope into consideration, Randy held a few inches below the bull's spine and squeezed the trigger. True to the calculations, the bullet struck 6 inches below point of aim, producing a center hit. Remaining velocity was 1260 fps.

SIGHTING-IN SCOPES

A scope is a very useful hunting tool. Most shooters don't realize the true value of the optical advantage and light-gathering ability of a quality scope until their eyes get a little older. A riflescope has a front lens, the one facing the game, called the objective lens. The rear lens, the one you look through, is called the ocular lens. Scopes today allow you to adjust the scope's internal crosshairs by turning the turret adjustment screws.

If you've never mounted or sighted in a scope before, it's quite all right to have your dealer do it for you. If you want to do it yourself, you can sight in your gun without firing a shot. Many shooters use a collimator, a device that "boresights" by aligning the bore with a screen for crosshair adjustment. Simmons' 1481B Boresighter Kit comes with a collimator and 15 arbors that fit 17- through 50-caliber guns. Once the scope is boresighted and you have determined eye relief (usually about 3-1/2 inches), loosen the ocular lock ring and adjust the ocular ring counterclockwise until the crosshairs look fuzzy. Now back-focus until the hairs are sharp and tighten the lock ring again. This adjusts the scope for your master or aiming eye.

Start the sighting-in process at 25 yards. With most scopes, one click will move bullet impact 1/4-inch at 100 yards. But remember that at 25 yards that adjustment is quadrupled, meaning that it will take four clicks to move impact 1/4 inch at 25 yards. For example, if the initial three-shot group is two inches low and one inch left at 25 yards you need to move the vertical adjustment knob 32 clicks up and the wind age adjustment 16 clicks to the right to be on target at 100 yards. Always shoot three-shot groups before making an adjustment. Due to interior design, some scopes will not always follow the adjustment you made until a shot has been fired. Further sighting-in and adjustments should be made at your various hunting ranges. Sighting-in should be conducted on a stable bench rest. And remember: make certain that all scope mount screws are tight.

6

The Blackpowder Shotgun

In the pre-dawn darkness, a fading moon and crystal clear sky hinted at a perfect October day. The hemlock-clad hillside I had just ascended was well-populated with roosted turkeys. The treetops of the hemlocks below me and the oaks above me became clear as daylight approached. The clucks and putts of elevated birds soon let me know that I was sitting within hearing distance of three different flocks. As the birds awoke, I waited for just the right moment to scrape the lid of my box call across the side rails. The flock in the hemlocks below was the first to react. After only 10 minutes of coaxing, the turkeys headed in my direction as I sat looking over the barrel of my blackpowder shotgun. A large hen led the way. I touched off the blackpowder scattergun when a bird stepped from behind a tree at 30 yards. What a morning!

Sadie, the author's 10-year-old springer spaniel, has literally been brought up as a blackpowder bird dog. These partridge and woodcock were taken with a Dixie Gun Works 20-ga. double featuring an open cylinder bore in the right barrel and a slightly tighter improved cylinder in the left.

RAISED ON SHOTGUNS

Upland game hunting with double-barreled shotguns was part of my family long before I appeared on the scene. My grandfather used a muzzleloading double as a youth over a century ago. As a youngster, I was introduced to hunting with a 20-ga. shotshell double by hunting squirrels and cottontails. In my teens I progressed to white rabbits, partridges, woodcock, pheasants and waterfowl. It has been 30 years since the passing of my grandfather. But I know for certain that he would be amused if he saw my father and me open our gun cases today.

Deer hunting and special seasons breathed new life into blackpowder shooting and put muzzleloading rifles back in business. Since the early 1970s I have been consumed by the blackpowder challenge and have hunted whitetails, caribou, elk, pronghorn, mule deer, moose and bear. About a decade ago, the first muzzleloading shotgun joined our blackpowder battery. The appeal was instant.

Squirrels, rabbits, upland birds, and wild turkeys began to provide more hunting action in one outing than the whitetail could in a whole season. My springer spaniel has been literally brought up as a blackpowder bird dog. Looking back, I can't believe I waited so long to get into front-loading shotguns after so many years of great scattergun hunts and memories. These smoothbore throwbacks to an earlier day have given me more hunting seasons, more time afield, more shooting opportunities, more interaction with game, and a new appreciation for the good, old-fashioned fun that can be had with a blackpowder shotgun.

There is a definite pride in bagging an autumn turkey with an authentic, traditional shotgun like this Tennessee Valley Muzzleloading 20-ga./62-cal. flintlock fowler.

Powder, wads, shot, and over-shot card compose the loading chain of the blackpowder shotgun. Shooting accessories include T/C's U-View capper, powder measure and powder flask and a shot pouch from Dixie Gun Works.

THE BASIC SHOOTING IRON

The blackpowder shotgun is a pretty basic shooting iron. It is literally a lock, a stock, and a smoothbore barrel. Percussion shotguns dominate the market. Like the rifle, the muzzleloading shotgun requires a full knowledge of its operation and handling. You should first read the shotgun's manual and master its mechanics. After disassembling, cleaning, and reassembling the shotgun, it's time to gather shooting components and head for the shooting range. Components should include:

PROPELLANT: Goex or Elephant brand blackpowder in FFg granulation or Pyrodex RS or Select.

WADS: fiber or felt lubricated wads to cushion the shot charge and separate it from the powder. (I have never been a fan of fussing with plastic shot cups in a muzzleloading shotgun.)

SHOT: of a size and material appropriate to the game.

OVER-SHOT CARDS: thin discs of felt, cardboard or foam to be firmly seated on top of the load shot.

Before loading the muzzleloading shotgun for the first time after it has sat idle, wipe its bore to remove any oil, moisture or fouling, and then snap a few percussion caps on it if it's a caplock, or clean its vent with a pick if it's a flintlock. This ensures a clean, dry flash channel to the main barrel charge. Now you're ready to load.

If your shotgun is a caplock, put the hammer at half-cock or leave the breech port open to allow trapped air to escape from the barrel during loading. If you're shooting a flintlock, leave your vent pick in place to form an air pocket in the powder charge. With the shotgun butt on the ground and its barrel tilted away from your body, pour a premeasured powder charge down the barrel, firmly seat a cushion wad on top of the powder charge, and pour a premeasured shot charge down the barrel. Now seat an over-shot wad or card firmly on top of the shot.

If shooting a double-barrel shotgun, employ a method that makes certain of which barrel is being loaded in order to avoid double-charging a barrel. My father and I always place the ramrod in the opposing barrel during the loading process. (Just as we mark a ramrod with witness marks to indicate empty or charged status, leaving the ramrod in the charged barrel helps us remember which barrel we're charging). Lastly, with the gun pointed in a safe direction, place a 209 shotgun primer in the breech port, a percussion cap on the nipple, or put a priming charge in the flash pan. You're now ready to shoot.

A blackpowder shotgun must be patterned for the intended type of hunting, just as a muzzleloading rifle must be sighted in. Range time not only lets you know how the gun shoots, but gives you a hands-on familiarity with the shotgun in action. Considerations during shot pattern testing include a) center of pattern vs. point of aim and b) density and consistency of pattern at the shooting distance desired. A close-quarters brush gun for woodcock and grouse is not going to be patterned the same as a goose or turkey gun. The effectiveness of a shotgun load depends on adequate pellet energy and shot pattern in relation to the size of the game hunted.

PATTERN PROOFING

Shot patterns are determined mostly by the constriction at the barrel's muzzle called the choke. Patterning is done on large 4-foot square cardboard or plywood backers, with 3-foot square sheets of paper tacked on to record each pattern tested. Chokes are determined by test patterns in 30-inch circles at 40 yards. A full choke should put at least 70 percent of the pellets into the 30-inch circle, a modified choke should produce a 50 percent pattern, an improved cylinder a 40 percent pattern, and the

Shot used by hunters today include (top row) Hevi-Shot and Lead. (Bottom row) Steel, Tungsten Matrix, and Copper-clad Lead.

Waterfowl hunters require shotguns such as this Dixie 10-ga. magnum with chrome-lined barrels to handle harder, non-toxic shot.

no-choke cylinder bore, a 30 percent pattern. For realistic field expectations, a shotgun should shoot a 70 percent pattern into the 30-inch circle at the following distances: a full choke barrel at 40 yards, a modified choke at 35 yards, an improved cylinder choke at 30 yards, and a cylinder bore at 25 yards. For example, a 1-oz. charge of #6 shot contains around 225 pellets. A 70 percent pattern would place almost 180 pellets in the 30-inch circle. It has been said that the full choke is a demanding mistress, while the improved cylinder is a forgiving friend.

Today, with manufacturer's guidelines, much of the guesswork concerning load patterning and testing has been eliminated. The traditional loading method for muzzleloading shotguns has been volume-for-volume of powder and shot. The volume equivalent of 70 gr. FFg or Pyrodex is 1 oz. of shot. In many guns, good patterns are still derived from this method. Slightly more shot than powder often provides the best pattern. But only through experimentation will you appreciate how how a light load disperses shot rapidly, while a heavier charge holds pellets together for longer shots. And as is true of blackpowder rifles, shotgun loads can reach the point of diminishing returns. Too strong a charge can literally shoot holes through a pattern.

WHAT CHARGE? WHAT SHOT SIZE?

Matching the load to your intended game and shooting conditions is your first consideration. Are you shooting grouse, pheasants, woodcock and quail over a bird dog, jump-shooting puddle ducks, pass-shooting doves, ambushing white rabbits or cottontails behind beagles, dusting squirrels out of trees, whaling away at geese over decoys, or enticing turkeys to the call? While some game loads overlap, others have a distinct purpose. Whereas lead shot is the norm for upland game, steel, tungsten, bismuth or Hevi-Shot is required for waterfowl. Waterfowl require not only stiff powder charges around 80 to 100 grains for distance and velocity, but shotguns with barrels that can handle the harder shot in sizes up to #2 or BB. This shooter demand sparked its own new market of blackpowder shotguns with chrome-lined barrels to handle the new non-toxic shot.

Don't draw the conclusion that smaller shot size creates a better pattern. My father's cylinder bore 20-guage flintlock fowler, loaded with 70 grains of FFFg, two felt overpowder wads, and one overshot wad, produced a better pattern with one ounce of #5 shot than it did with the same measure of #9 shot at 25 yards. We got better patterns out of a single barreled 12-gauge for both upland game and turkey loads with the modified screw-in choke rather than the full, as one would expect. To date, the most impressive patterning results my father and I ever achieved were produced by a modern styled in-line turkey gun. A 12-ga. Knight MK-86–loaded with 100 gr. of Pyrodex Select, three felt cushion wads, 2 oz. of copper plated #6 shot, and a thin foam over-shot wad–produced a 95 percent pattern with 450 pellets at 40 yards. There were 96 pellets in the turkey head in the middle of the patterning circle target.

In his *Gun Digest Blackpowder Reloading Manual*, Sam Fadala tested 10 blackpowder shotguns, ranging from single barrel 20-gauges to 10-ga. doubles to the modern 12-ga. Knight MK-86. All propelled the variety of shot charges at around 1000 fps velocity. Dixie Gun Work's black powder loading data for 20-, 12-, and 10-ga. muzzleloading shotguns also show similar results: a 20-gauge loaded with 55 gr. FFg and 3/4 oz. of shot achieved 992 fps, while a 10-ga. loaded with 100 gr. FFg and 1-½ oz. shot made 1033 fps.

A good way to test shot velocity and the effective range of your patterned load is to set a clay pigeon against a solid backstop such as a sand bank. Start at your optimum patterned range, say 25 yards with an improved cylinder, and shoot the clay pigeon. By stepping back five yards with each shot, you will determine what range your pellets no longer inflict enough damage to the clay target to be effective on game in the field.

An important consideration for shotgun accuracy is center of pattern vs. point of aim.

VERSATILE AND FUN

Shooting the blackpowder shotgun takes a little more discipline than shooting a conventional scattergun. The lock time on a muzzleloading shotgun is slower than its modern counterpart. The shooter has to learn to stay with the target longer. In the case of wing shooting, that also means getting on the target sooner to allow you the time for your hold and follow-through. In W.W. Greener's 1881 book *The Gun*, he discusses the use of staying on target with the blackpowder shotgun. Greener emphasized visually picking up the bird's flight, instinctively shouldering the gun and bringing it up on the bird from below or behind, firing at the moment of proper lead and not stopping your swing to lose the line of flight. Today, the best way for a new blackpowder shotgunner to get the hang of it, and for a seasoned shooter to stay in tune, is to practice on flying clay birds released from a manual trap or at the skeet range.

One of my favorite shotguns is a Dixie Gun Works 20-ga. double. The first autumn I used it my father and I shot woodcock, grouse and quail with 60 gr. of FFg pushing 1 oz. of #8 shot. We shot pheasants with 70 gr. of FFg behind 1 oz. of #6 shot. And we shot turkeys using the tighter choked improved cylinder left barrel with the same pheasant load. Our DGW 10-ga. double is tops for traditional turkey and other stout birds. Single-barrel 12-gauges such as the Thompson/Center New Englander and the CVA Trapper are easy to shoot, simple to use blackpowder shotguns. My father thoroughly enjoys his authentic single barrel flintlock fowler made by Tennessee Valley Muzzleloading. Besides upland game and autumn wild turkeys, he has even shot deer with the 20-ga./62-caliber smooth bore. The flintlock shoots an amazing three shot, 3-inch group at 50 yards with a .015-patched 60-caliber round ball pushed by 70 gr. of FFFg. Being a shotgun, the flintlock has no rear sight and a traditional turtle-style, blade front sight. The velocity of the almost 300-gr. pumpkin ball is around 1100 fps.

The clay pigeon test is the best way to determine the effective range of your patterned load for upland game, waterfowl, or wild turkeys.

ACCESSORIES

A priming device, be it a capper or priming flask, and premeasured powder and shot charges are essential accessories for a blackpowder shotgun hunter. You must never pour powder from a bulk container into the barrel of a blackpowder gun. If a spark is lingering somewhere in the barrel, it can turn your bulk container into a hand grenade. So use a powder measure to load from a flask or container–it has much less potential for trouble. As a shotgun hunter, you'll need a shot dipper to measure your charges as well as wads and over-shot cards. For shotgun hunters there are volumetric measures that allow for equal measures of both powder and shot. In the hunting field today the pre-load and speed loader are king. They are efficient and, more importantly, safe. Accessories such as a nipple wrench for the caplock, extra flints for the flintlock, and a few ramrod attachments and patches will help eliminate problems afield if they ever arise. These accessories easily fit into a hunting vest pocket or a small belt pouch.

A WORD FROM THE WISE

I recently had the opportunity to talk with Dr. Andy Baker, a four-time National Muzzleloader Skeet Champion. Dr. Baker has competed in the National Muzzle Loading Rifle Association shoots in Friendship, Ind., since 1957. Dr. Baker shared with me what he considers the most important points of successful muzzleloader shotgun shooting.

1) Gun Fit: Close both your eyes, mount the gun, and then open your eyes. The barrel beads should align.

2) Shoot Instinctively: Never see the barrels. Let the eyes rule by looking where you want the gun to go. Lock your eyes on the "target."

3) Follow the line of the bird. Make sure your muzzle has passed through the bird. "Butt-Belly-Beak-Bang!" Never ever halt your swing. Keep those barrels moving! When a bird is flushed, cast your eyes ahead of the airborne target as your barrels will naturally catch your eyes. Noted shooting instructor Jack Mitchell of Cornwall, England, says, "Speed is lead and lead is speed."

4) Remember to adjust your swing. Live birds accelerate while clay targets decelerate.

5) Shot pattern is one thing. Shot string is another. Shot flies in an elongated string like a swarm of bees that is about 6 to 8 feet long. The idea is to rake your target with the shot string. This is why "lead" is so important and often hard to grasp for many shooters. All of the shot does not get to the target at the same time.

On the subject of regulating cylinder bore shotguns, Dr. Baker feels that lubricated cushion wads are as important as the powder and the shot. The thicker the cushion wad, the more open the pattern. The thinner the cushion wads, the tighter the pattern. To improve shot velocity and get optimum lubrication out of cushion wads, Dr. Baker recommends the use of a thin .125 or 1/8-inch card wad over the powder, then a lubricated cushion wad behind the shot. Then top off the load with a thin card overshot wad. This loading procedure is very beneficial to hunters firing many shots in the course of a day as it keeps fouling to a minimum, enhances loading, and provides consistent patterns.

Dr. Andy Baker's saying, "Butt-Belly-Beak-Bang," makes certain that your muzzle passes through the flying target.

Two-compartment speed loaders for powder and shot, and film canisters for wads, are an efficient way to carry your loading components afield. Note the inline capper on lanyard for easy access.

The blackpowder shotgun is easy to swab clean as it is a true smoothbore.

A common gripe against blackpowder firearms concerns the necessity of cleaning them. The shotgun is easy to clean, however, because it's a smooth bore: no lands or grooves to harbor all that nasty, corrosive fouling. Whether you prefer or one of the specially-formulated blackpowder solvents, the cleaning process is as simple as swabbing the bore. Just remove the barrel from the stock and go to town with your cleaning rod. In stubborn cases I use a bore brush to loosen fouling and a patch over the brush to swab the barrel clean. I also use a pipe cleaner to clean the flash hole, the nipple, and the vent, and I make sure to give all metal surfaces a thin coat of anti-corrosion lubricant. This makes it necessary to wipe the bore clean of any oil before future loading, but it's well worth the extra trouble.

ENHANCING YOUR SHOTGUN SHOOTING SKILLS

Gil and Vicki Ash, proprietors of the Optimum Shotgun Performance Shooting School, have just released a new video titled *14 Tips To Better Shotgun Hunting*. This new sporting clays video is a collection of the most common problems Gil and Vicki have seen among thousands of shooters of all ability and experience levels, along with their solutions for overcoming those problems. The topics covered include the six most frequent mechanical causes for misses; patterning your gun for fit; when and why to shoot with a mounted gun; how to "slow down" targets; grip, stance, and balance and how they control consistency; three reasons shooters miss targets they know how to hit; risks of different shooting methods; and home practice.

When I received this video I thought, "What can a sporting clays video do for me?" The answer proved to be "plenty." From barrel awareness to tempo and timing for a smooth swing, to the home practice technique with a MagLite flashlight slipped into your barrel of your shotgun, Gil and Vicki made me aware of my failings and provided

answers that have made me a better muzzleloading shotgun shooter. For more information contact: OSP Shooting School, www.ospschool.com, 15050 Cutten Rd., Houston, Texas, 77070, 800-838-7533.

Optimum Shotgun Performance Shooting School Instructors Gil and Vicki Ash will make you a better wing shooter with their *14 Tips to Better Shotgunning.*

The heritage, challenge, and hands-on approach of turkey hunting are a perfect match for muzzleloading shotguns like the Dixie Gun Works 10-ga. magnum.

Wild turkey hunting has brought about a revived interest in blackpowder shotguns. Modern style shotguns like this scoped Knight TK2000 and the Thompson/Center Encore with fiber-optic sights were designed specifically for turkey hunting and appeal to many hunters.

GIVE IT A TRY

The true hunting experience is what many sportsman are seeking as we enter a new century. More and more shotgun hunters are discovering a renewed sense of achievement by creating a load, built up layer by layer inside a barrel, using a ramrod. The hunter that uses a frontstuffing scattergun on flying birds, running small game, and wild turkey is definitely a hunter interested in a quality experience. If you like muzzleloader hunting but want more action than a one-shot deer hunt, consider the fun and versatile blackpowder shotgun.

TURKEY SHOTGUNS: PRIDE AND PREFERENCE

What the whitetail deer did for the resurgence of the muzzleloader hunting rifle in the last 30 years, the wild turkey has done for the muzzleloading shotgun during the last fifteen. Spring or fall, the muzzleloading tradition of hunting wild turkeys is fun and contagious. More hunters every year find themselves calling spring and fall birds within range of their favorite style of primitive scattergun. I took my first wild turkey while looking through the hammers of a double-barreled 10-ga. Since that time, success has come with other muzzleloading shotguns including a 20-ga. flintlock fowler, a 20-ga. double, various single-barrel 12-gauge caplocks, and a modern styled in-line 12-ga. made specifically for the turkey hunter.

For many, hunting the wild turkey takes some getting used to. Finding yourself in your favorite hunting grounds in the spring of the year seems odd. But once you began to learn the ways of the wild turkey, the spring woodlands take on new meaning. You'll find yourself looking for dusting areas in dry, sandy soil with feathers scattered about and scratching areas where turkeys scrape the ground looking for food. With experience, you'll be able to distinguish hen droppings (roundish) from gobbler droppings (J-shaped), and you'll learn to read their tracks in soft woodland grounds or cultivated.

Muzzleloader turkey hunters do so for three reasons: heritage and the increased challenge of the hunt; appre-

Load testing for shot pattern density and effective range is a vital step in achieving a lethal headshot on a gobbler.

Center's New Englander and more recent Black Mountain Magnum 12-gauges have traditional features and feel but are technically non-replicas as they resemble no particular shooting irons of old. Guns such as the Black Mountain Magnum possess modern gun characteristics including synthetic stocks and fiber-optic sights. And then there's the most modern turkey muzzleloading shotgun, the Knight MK-86, a synthetic stocked, single-barrel, in-line plunger ignition shotgun with an extra-full screw-in choke.

Every one of these shotguns is capable of taking a turkey. There is a tremendous sense of achievement bagging fall birds over decoys as my father has done with the flintlock fowler. Single barrel muzzleloaders are light to carry and easy to manage and shoot. Having read Dwain Bland's articles and his *Turkey Hunter's Digest* over the years, I didn't think there was any other way to hunt a wild turkey than with a double-barrel hammer gun. And as turkey hunting's popularity has resulted in more hunters calling at birds in the woods, I have come to appreciate a tightly-choked, scoped modern shotgun when smart, silent toms let the hens lead the way, standing their ground 35 to 40 yards away.

But as is true of all hunting guns, the turkey shotgun must also have a personal appeal to the shooter, whether it be the gun's historical appeal, its balance and feel, or its suitability for the job at hand. When a muzzleloader hunter selects a turkey shotgun, he must find an acceptable balance between pride and preference.

CHOICES, CHOICES

Seeing as how he has always been more interested in a quality experience than bag limits, I wasn't surprised when my father began hunting wild turkeys with a muzzleloader in 1991. His gun of choice was the Dixie Gun Works 10-ga. magnum shotgun. After load testing and patterning the muzzleloading scattergun, he arrived at a powder and shot charge that maintained its density for a good 30-yard pattern out of the left modified-choke barrel. After several frustrating turkey hunts, like the time a gobbler came into calling and stopped behind a stump, my father finally found muzzleloading turkey success with his load of 90 gr. of FFg blackpowder, two Ox-Yoke Wonder Wads, 1-1/2 oz. of #5 shot, and an overshot card. I, too, was initiated into muzzleloader turkey hunting with the DGW 10-gauge.

Since that time our turkey-hunting arsenal has grown. We have a few muzzleloaders that we take hunting both spring and fall. For each of these shotguns, we have determined killing turkey loads through patient trial and load patterning, keeping in mind that, in turkey hunting, head shots are the rule of the day. Our Tennessee Valley Muzzleloading 20-ga. flintlock fowler works best with 70 gr. of FFFg blackpowder, two Wonder Wads, 1 oz. of copper-plated #6 shot, and one Wonder Wad over the shot. Our Thompson/Center 12-ga. New Englander does best

ciation of the hands-on approach that makes the gunner accountable for everything from gun preparation to ignition; and the fact that both turkey hunting and muzzleloading hunting are strictly hands-on propositions.

A successful gobbler hunt is created a step at a time. The most popular tactic is luring spring mating season gobblers into range. This is accomplished by locating a tom, employing a calling strategy and a variety of hunting tactics as needed, and, finally, making a shot within your muzzleloader's effective limits.

There are many muzzleloading shotgun styles to choose from. A Tennessee Valley Muzzleloading 20-ga./62-cal. flintlock fowler owned by my father and me is a handsome, true replica of the original smoothbore guns. Our 10- and 20-ga. Dixie Gun Works doubles possess a striking resemblance to the hammer guns of the latter half of the nineteenth century. The CVA Trapper, Thompson/

with 100 gr. of Pyrodex Select, two Wonder Wads, 1-3/8 oz. of #5 shot with one Wonder Wad over the shot. And lastly, we have the Knight, MK 86 12 gauge shotgun with a Simmons Whitetail Classic 2 x 32 scope. This shotgun shoots incredibly tight, dense patterns out to 40 yards with a load of 100 gr. of Pyrodex Select, three Wonder Wads, 2 oz. of copper plated #6 shot, and a thin foam wad over the shot. This load in the Knight MK-86 has become the yardstick by which we measure all other loads.

The Dixie 10 ga. and the Knight MK-86 have become our preferred spring guns. The TVM Fowler is about as traditional a turkey-shooting gun for a fall hunt as you could ask for to take that Thanksgiving bird. Other good turkey guns my father and I have tested and hunted with include CVA's Trapper 12-ga. shotgun, the Navy Arms T&T (Trap and Turkey) 12-ga. double, Cabela's 10-ga. double with interchangeable chokes, T/C's Black Mountain Magnum shotgun, and Traditions' Turkey Pro In-line 12 gauge.

Last year we put the T/C Encore 12-ga. with a full-choke turkey tube barrel to the test. It was a novelty to us. In the past, we have fired flintlocks, hammer guns and plunger-ignited shotguns fired with priming powder, #11 percussion caps, musket caps, and 209 shotgun primers. But the Encore was our first break-action shotgun. The 209-shotgun primer breech plug is easily removed for straight-through cleaning. Excellent fiber-optic sights and the matte-finish Realtree Hardwood camo pattern on barrel and stock make this shotgun look like it's really in the turkey business. It took only three shots to proof this short, handy modern-style hammer gun. We put the Encore to our yardstick MK-86 test with 100 gr. of FFg blackpowder, two Wonder Wads overpowder wads, 2 oz. of #6 copper-plated shot, and one overshot wad. No sight adjustment was necessary as the Encore fired two excellent patterns at 30 yards, and a very good pattern at 40.

BRINGING IT ALL TOGETHER

Muzzleloading shotguns are a fun and rewarding way to take a tom turkey whether you are a novice or seasoned turkey hunter. This past spring I gave the T/C Encore 12-ga. shotgun a try on toms. On a late May morning after listening to two birds gobble at daybreak from their roosts, I set up decoys at the edge of the woods near the corner of a clearing. I took a secluded position in a briar patch and just waited. Around 9 a.m., two toms worked towards me in the sparse springtime woods. As soon as the lead bird saw the decoys, he fanned and strutted right in. I let the gobbler close to 20 yards before I let the single barrel scattergun rip. Bird down.

Like many, I had enjoyed turkey hunting for years and had taken several birds. But it wasn't until I had looked between the hammers of a DGW 10-ga. double barrel at a really big gobbler at 30 yards that this spring turkey thing really grabbed me. There is nothing quite like a big impressive tom strutting into a sunlit opening in full display. When you first see that magnificent bird with tail fanned, chest puffed, primary wing feathers dragging the ground, and a red, white, and blue head, you have all you can do to keep your cool. But when the bird takes two or three quick steps in your direction and emits the mating gobbler's spit-and-drum, *pffftt duuuuuuuum*, it is truly one of hunting's magical moments. Whether you're holding a flintlock fowler, a double-barrel hammer gun, or a modern style muzzleloader, you'll see why more people are discovering blackpowder turkey guns.

HEVI-SHOT

It's a familiar April routine for my father and me: going to the range and patterning our muzzle-loading turkey loads. On this day we were trying the non-toxic shot called Hevi-Shot. This shot, unlike others, is composed of tungsten, nickel, and iron to create a density of 12 grams per cubic centimeter, which makes Hevi-Shot "heavier than lead [11.2 gr./cc]." With steel pellets at 7.9 gr./cc and bismuth at 9.7, Hevi-Shot is the first lead substitute to offer density and downrange energy equal to or superior to lead. Due to its manufacturing process, Hevi-Shot is formed as odd, irregularly-shaped blobs. Because of its density, smaller size shot in smaller amounts, as compared to lead, is recommended. For example, #6 Hevi-Shot is ballisticlly equivalent to the lead #4 or #5 found in most turkey loads. In our T/C Encore 12-gauge, we usually shoot 2 oz. of copper-plated lead #6 shot over 100 gr. Pyrodex RS. For a Hevi-Shot load, we used 1-5/8 oz. of their new #6 shot. Knight shot cups were trimmed down to accommodate the shot charge, and a foam over-shot wad topped off the seated load.

At the patterning boards, our new Hevi-Shot loads were extremely tight. Turkeys out to 40 yards would be in trouble with that non-toxic but lethal swarm screaming toward them.

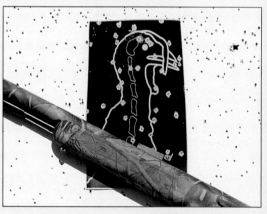

7

You Can't Miss with Special Season Muzzleloading!

"The whitetail is a shrewd, wary, knowing beast; but it owes its prolonged stay in the land chiefly to the fact that it is an inveterate skulker, and fond of the thickest cover."

Theodore Roosevelt, The Wilderness Hunter, *1893.*

If you like muzzleloader hunting and whitetail deer, you couldn't be living at a better time. During the last decade I have bought licenses and applied for permits to muzzleloader hunt for whitetail deer multiple times in seven states and a Canadian province. In 1977, my own state of New York started its Northern Zone Adirondack region hunt, a seven-day period during the third week of October. I have never missed hunting at least part of this annual special season.

This Adirondack ritual will always remain the foundation of my muzzleloader deer hunting. It is in this land where the whitetail deer taught me how to hunt. A land where post-Revolutionary War hunters Nick Stoner and Nat Foster recorded incredible deer kills with their $70.00 double-shooters made by Willis Avery. A land where still-hunting a deer trail with a traditional muzzleloader across your arm just feels right. A land where both buck and doe are legal and success or failure determined by effort and skill.

One of my best lessons in my formative muzzleloading years happened while tracking a deer on a skiff of snow. I was so intent on the tracks that I couldn't believe my eyes when I came upon the 6-point buck a half hour later. At first I just saw football shapes of beech leaves. They were the ears of the deer watching me on his back trail. I was so enthralled by my tracking accomplishment that I completely blundered the shot. But the rare early

October snow conditions persisted and I tracked down a doe two days later. This time, however, I picked my opening in the whips and placed my shot. I had my first deer with a muzzleloader.

Although I found success during the late '70s and early '80s by still-hunting and taking does, it took me several years to bag my first good buck in a land with fewer than 15 deer per square mile. Today, my home state also has a late muzzleloader season in the southern half of the state where a larger deer population offers an excellent primitive arms opportunity. This past season both a coyote and a whitetail were in the sights of my traditional style Virginia rifle during the December hunt.

By the late "80s I began adding an out-of-state deer hunt to my muzzleloader hunting. The first time I muzzleloader deer hunted out of state, I went to Kentucky where my tag was good for buck or doe. On this trip I rattled in a buck to my Storey sidehammer and my father took a late hunt doe with a "new" Knight rifle. It was a novel experience hunting in a land where deer were so plentiful. Next came Illinois, where I saw more bucks on two different hunts in the land of Lincoln than I had seen in my life at home. The most memorable was an aggressive 10-pointer that I rattled in. The buck had fought so much that he only had stubs for points. In the '90s I hunted Missouri twice and enjoyed just being in such deer active woods. But a dud cap spelled heartbreak on an outstanding buck. In the late '90s I hunted Iowa twice.

A winter whitetail during a Pennsylvania flintlock hunt is just one of the "special season" opportunities afforded muzzleloader hunters today.

Limited permit drawings in a land of phenomenal habitat produce big, old bucks. My father and I both got our best muzzleloader bucks to date in Iowa.

But the out-of-state hunt that I have returned to six times–a hunt that tests the skills, stamina, and patience of die-hard muzzleloader hunters–is Pennsylvania's flintlock hunt. The post-Christmas weather in northwestern part of the state in the lee of the Great Lakes is unpredictable. We have hunted in rain, sleet, mud, and shirtsleeves. But on a sub-zero morning plowing through 30 inches of snow in 1997, I snow-shoed to a hemlock bedding area on the side of a hardwood ridge. A deer taken that bitter, awful day with a Dixie Deerslayer rifle rates among my most rewarding muzzleloading accomplishments.

It's no secret that the whitetail deer is a wildlife management success story. The North American Indians ate their meat, wore their skins, and traded their hides to the Europeans for knives, clothing, and other trade goods. As settlers moved in on both sides of the Appalachians, more than a century of unrestricted market hunting and habitat destruction decimated a pre-colonial population estimated at over 20 million. By 1900 our whitetail population had dwindled to a half-million and hunting was curtailed in many regions. Bag limits and "bucks only" hunting began the restoration of the whitetail.

Today, we have a whitetail deer population in the neighborhood of the original 20 million as a result of a

Special season muzzleloader hunts serve game management purposes while providing quality hunting for primitive arms hunters.

century of well-controlled conservation and game management programs. That the whitetail has done so well is reflected in recent headlines such as "Bulging Deer Herd Wreaks Havoc On Indiana Crops." According to this late 1990s article the Indiana Department of Natural Resources was dealing with a deer population that was taking a toll on the state's corn and subsequent insurance industry; however, the deer remained valued as a resource in the

Whitetail populations have rebounded beyond all expectations, creating tremendous muzzleloader hunting opportunities.

state due to the economic impact that hunting brings in the form of store revenues and tourism. And this scenario is the same to some extent in every state the whitetail deer calls home.

The carrying capacity of any given area for deer is when the deer herd has sufficient food in its habitat to survive the winter. When they don't, the deer move into agricultural lands or into the gardens and shrubberies of sprawling communities. The "cultural carrying capacity" is a new term coined by a Connecticut deer biologist a few years ago. It defines the actual number of deer that is desired, or that will be tolerated, by the people who own the land the deer live on. To manage the expanding whitetail populations, state game and conservation departments across this country depended upon regular firearm seasons to control numbers. Then bow hunting

A limited permit draw in Iowa's quality buck country resulted in a memorable hunt for father and son.

was added to enhance the challenge and increase the deer take. During the last 25 years, the management tool of muzzleloader whitetail hunting was a welcomed addition. If you haven't noticed, the good old days of muzzleloader hunting are now!

Special muzzleloader seasons began popping up in the 1960s and 1970s when wildlife management agencies began instituting more hunting opportunities to control our growing deer populations. Today, almost all of the 50 states have at least one muzzleloader hunt. In a recent survey, only three states had a decline in muzzleloader permits, while 29 states had an increase. At last count, there were 1,115,781 resident muzzleloader licenses sold across the country. Michigan leads the nation with 173,000 muzzleloader hunters. But it is West Virginia's muzzleloader hunters that account for highest percentage of their state's total deer harvest with 16%.

Most muzzleloader hunting seasons fall before or after regular firearm and bow seasons. Pennsylvania's two-week flintlock season has always been the two weeks following Christmas. Pennsylvania now schedules a three-day antlerless deer hunt in October due to the substantial number of hunters who expressed an interest in an earlier season as well. Other states with booming deer populations such as Texas have a one-week antlerless muzzleloader season

in mid January. Arkansas, where the total deer harvest has tripled in the last 15 years, enforces quality deer management with a statewide minimum on bucks with three points on a side.

It is an admirable accomplishment to tag a cagey, rack buck. The traditional emphasis on a deer wearing antlers is engrained in all deer hunters. Many older hunters grew up when it was legal to shoot only an antlered deer. Many younger hunters today are swept away with the all-consuming trophy buck mentality. And these new hunters miss the point that consistent trophy hunters were deer hunters first–hunters who learned the woodcraft and muzzleloader skills to hunt deer and make killing shots on bucks and does. Hey, who at some time in their muzzleloader-hunting career wouldn't like to bag a really nice whitetail buck?

But for those whose hunt in the real world with booming doe populations and a high percentage of 1-½-year-old bucks, antlerless deer hunting is their best shot at success. Wildlife managers have proven time and time again the importance of taking does as well as bucks.

Special season muzzleloading not only gives you the opportunity to become a better hunter, but an accomplished hunter with primitive arms. Try it. You can't miss!

8

Blackpowder Barometer Bucks

Whitetail hunters have long been aware of the effects of weather on whitetails. Due to time constraints or storm duration, deer hunters often get to experience only a portion of a weather front. During one of my December hunts, a narrow but strong storm front marched across the state of Iowa. The abrupt changes in weather during a 24-hour period gave me a unique opportunity to see, and feel, every sequence of the passing front. It also allowed for hunters to see the pre-storm, peak storm, and post-storm effect on whitetail activity after a long stretch of warm, balmy weather. For the muzzleloader hunters in one southern Iowa camp, the storm will long be remembered for more than snow, sleet, and freezing rain.

The memorable hunt in question occurred in the Iowa shotgun season from December 5 to December 12. Steve Shoop promoted the hunt at his J&S Trophy Hunts, Sundown Lake Lodge, as a muzzleloader hunt. I was greatly looking forward to hunting Iowa after receiving one of the limited draw permits. Thirteen muzzleloader hunters pursuing whitetails on 9300 acres of managed farm country sounded promising, but the abnormally warm autumn had been challenging for Shoop's 47 bow hunters. Still, they put 14 bucks into the Pope & Young record book, with most success coming at dawn and dusk. Mother nature can play an important role in the outcome of a five-day hunt. Not even the outfitter was expecting the outcome of the weather's effect on this hunt.

A HUNT TO REMEMBER

Opening day was sunny and beautiful with a warm, sultry westerly breeze. Thin cirrus clouds streaked the sky. Tree stand hunters overlooked oak bottoms, food plots, and planted crops in comfort. Unfortunately, the deer were

This particular storm allowed hunters to see the effect of each phase of the weather front on the whitetails: the pre-storm feeding activity as the barometer fell, the bedded deer at the peak of the storm as the barometric pressure bottomed, and the frenzy of buck activity on the rising barometer during post storm period.

The storm rolled across southern Iowa with some impressive results.

as comfortable as the hunters. They didn't begin to stir until last light. As the sunset and darkness brought cooler temperatures, every food source became active with whitetails. Riding back to camp, hunters couldn't believe the amount of bucks and does that were seen crossing roads and standing in fields. Back at camp, the weather forecast showed a storm front rolling down through the Dakotas and into Iowa during the night. The forecast for morning was rain and snow.

Departing camp in the morning, many hunters complained of aching joints and old injuries. My father has a steel replacement knee that was singing the blues as he made his way to his ground blind. The first rays of sun cast a pinkish glow off the wall of frontal clouds on the western horizon. The sky was full of moving waterfowl and the breeze had shifted from the east. A 10-point buck hurried down the trail below my father. But a scrape doctored with Rickard's Rut Gel Lure caught the buck's attention. As the whitetail sniffed the treated overhanging branch, the crosshairs of a Simmons Aetec 2.8 to 10x44 settled on its shoulder. A squeeze of the trigger dropped the plunger on the hunter's .50 MK-85 Knight Hawk rifle. Two 50-gr. Pyrodex Pellets pushed off a 250-gr. all-copper Barnes sabot bullet. The first buck of the hunt went down just as the ceiling lowered and a line of dark rolling clouds unleashed a heavy downpour of rain.

The rain turned to sleet and came down in sheets. A cool wind picked up from the east. I had evacuated my tree stand and headed for the cover of some softwoods I had been eyeing. As I took refuge, I came upon three bedded does and a flock of turkeys that hadn't even left the roost that morning. The storm peaked and turned to a whiteout blizzard by mid-afternoon. At the last hour of daylight the storm let up, the temperature dropped, the wind resumed its northwesterly flow, and the whitetails came alive. I had taken a stand where the fingers of several oak bottoms rose to meet a large planted field. First it was a 6-pointer accompanied by does. Then an 8-pointer with does sprung out of another. A high brow-tined, 5-pointer reclaimed a scrape within 50 yards of me. When a wide 10-pointer followed 3 does along the edge of the woods 80 yards away, it was all this Adirondack whitetail hunter could take. I fired my own Knight MK-85 loaded with Pyrodex Pellets and a Barnes all-copper sabot bullet.

The hour after the storm was productive for two other hunters as well. Texas hunter Larry Weishuhn had a 14-pointer slip in behind him before he got the drop on the buck with a Knight 50-cal. T-Bolt Rifle using three 50-gr. Pyrodex Pellets and a 180-gr. Barnes Expander MZ sabot bullet. West Virginia hunter Romano Bergey took the opportunity to still-hunt the fresh snow and walked up on a large 10-pointer that he dropped with a 310-gr. sabot lead slug pushed by 100 gr. of blackpowder from a .54 LK-90 Knight rifle. Stars glistened through the breaks in the last of the cumulus and cirrus clouds in the cold December sky as successful hunters descended upon J&S's Sundown Lake Lodge.

By morning, the post-storm weather had completely taken over with clear, blue skies and 20-degree temperatures. Two Pennsylvania hunters would score on the backside of the storm. Barry Anderson was staying warm and still-hunting the new snow. At 8:45 he kicked up three does. Seventy yards from the does, a buck jumped to its feet in a thicket. Anderson settled his sights on the long-tined 9-pointer at 130 yards. John Pantuso was in his tree stand surrounded by three bedded bucks, two 8-pointers and a 6-point. When another buck cruised by whose body size and antlers dwarfed the other deer, he too lined up his sights and fired.

The results of the bucks taken around the storm period were astonishing. My father's 18-inch 10 pointer was the smallest. My 21-inch 10 pointer grossed 138 B&C. Bergey's buck grossed 157, Weishuhn's grossed 171, Anderson's scored 174, and Pantuso's measured 176 inches of antler. The cold spell kept the deer active the rest of the week. At the end of the five-day hunt, 10 hunters out of 13 were successful on rack bucks, including Tennessee hunter Brenda Valentine, who scored on a 150-class 10-pointer on the last evening. All participants agreed that this was a phenomenal hunt.

WEATHER FRONT WHITETAILS

We know that there are three periods of whitetail activity associated with storm fronts.

PRE-STORM activity is associated with whitetails traveling, with the emphasis on food. At this time hunters usually concentrate on food sources and the corridors that lead to them. As a front closes in, deer retreat to bedding areas. My father's buck was hurrying towards a bedding area with the approach of the ensuing storm. There were very few deer seen that morning by hunters. Pre-storm movements in the form of heavy feeding activity had occurred during the night, as witnessed by hunters returning to camp after sundown.

PEAK STORM activity consists of deer bedding down. The severity of the storm dictates the density of the cover taken to conserve energy and body heat. Hunting through these bedding areas is the only way to see these immobile whitetails.

POST-STORM activity will find deer leaving bedding areas to resume feeding. If it's during the rut, bucks will be reopening scrapes and covering their territory. This is a great time to still-hunt or stake out a proven point of travel, scrape line, or food source. During the Iowa hunt, five of the six successful storm front hunters scored during the post-storm period.

BAROMETRIC PRESSURE

Barometric pressure indicates air weight. Fronts are the boundaries between cold and warm air masses. The boundary lines on a weather map are called isobars, or lines of equal pressure. The difference in barometric pressure on each side of the isobar will determine the "high" and "low" pressure. Pressure measurements are essential for the plotting of isobars over the earth and for determining positions and movements of fronts. As atmospheric pressure differs according to elevation, all pressure readings are converted to what they would be if the readings were taken at sea level. This allows for accurate mapping of pressure readings anywhere in the world. Barometric pressure is divided on weather maps by isobars, calculated in millibars, and reported to us in inches of mercury, the most accurate form of measurement.

Humans recognize barometric pressure usually through discomfort. The hunters at Sundown Lake Lodge experienced aches and pains as the storm front approached. The old days of bunions foretelling impending weather weren't just wive's tales. The University of

Barometric pressure can tell you when to hunt and how to hunt.

Pennsylvania School of Medicine was one of the first to prove the effects of barometric pressure on humans. Thirty arthritic patients were put in sealed, room-sized climate chambers and exposed to simulated storm conditions. Dropped barometric pressures and boosted humidity levels produced stiffness and swelling in the patients' joints. Reversing the conditions brought immediate relief. Sinus pressure and pain due to changes in barometric pressure are proven and referred to as "cluster headaches" by the American Council for Headache Education. Jet lag, or fatigue, is the result of an extended pressure change. Today, doctors use hyperbaric and hypobaric chamber treatments for the "bends" from rapid diving and flying ascents and for problematic wound healing.

Barometric pressure is one of the leading indicators for forecasting weather. Fair weather is associated with a

Larry Weishuhn's buck was taken as the storm departed on a rising barometer.

steady or rising barometer. Stormy weather is associated with a steadily falling barometer. A telltale sign of a falling barometer is a ring around the moon. Weather clearing after a storm will find the barometer rapidly rising. Storm severity is often determined by how fast the barometer drops. A change in barometric pressure signals significant weather changes 18 to 48 hours prior to the weather's arrival.

What started merely as a blackpowder deer hunt became a lesson in barometric pressure and whitetail behavior for the successful hunters such as Brenda Valentine.

THE SUBTLE SIGNAL

Whereas humans feel winds shift, see clouds gather, and sense a pressure change on their bodies, whitetail deer have a built-in barometric sensor that triggers behavioral patterns. That is why deer cover that saw only routine travel from bedding to feeding areas suddenly sees a high traffic level one to two days before the arrival of a storm. Often even before precipitation begins, whitetails bed up and hold tight as the barometric pressure bottoms out. And even if snow or rain is still in the air, deer often become very active as soon as the barometric pressure starts rising again, signaling the end of the storm. The decisiveness of the whitetails' actions is definitely triggered by the severity of the rise or fall in barometric pressure.

The National Climatic Data Center has on record the barometric pressures in southern Iowa during our hunt. The pre-storm pressure was 29.81; then it rapidly dropped to 29.73 and quickly rose to 30.21. Meteorologist Scott Stevens at the NCDC states, "That is significant millibar movement." Illinois biologist Keith Thomas found the highest amount of whitetail feeding and movement occurred when barometric pressures were between 29.80 and 30.29. The results of the Iowa hunt certainly substantiated Thomas' research findings.

Barometric changes occur subtly, even imperceptibly, at first. That's where a barometer can come in handy.

PRESSURE = SUCCESS

Barometric pressure is a definite key to whitetail behavior. If you have done your homework, you will know where to hunt, when to be there, and whether you should take a stand and watch the action, or still-hunt to the deer. And to accomplish this, you need a barometer. A column of mercury that stands 30 inches high and exerts 1,016 millibars of pressure is the standard for measurement. But at 14 lbs. it is rather impractical for field use. But for hunters today there are compact weather meters that indicate exact barometric pressures and show weather trends as well. Two of the most popular are Cabela's compact 4 x 4-inch Jumbo Weather Forecaster and Lab Safety Supply's Pocket Weather Monitor. This unit records barometric pressure history for 12 hours and accurately forecasts for another 24.

Although I knew that weather fronts affected whitetail activity, I didn't become a firm believer in subtle barometric signals until I traveled to Iowa and hunted blackpowder barometer bucks.

9

Old Mountains – Old Traditions

"To the sportsman, whether of forest or flood, who has a taste of wilderness as god threw it from his hand, who loves the mountains, the old woods, romantic lakes and wild forest streams, this region is particularly inviting. "

S. H. Hammond, Wild Northern Scenes, 1857.

Today, the Adirondack Park consists of nearly 6 million acres of public and private lands in the northeastern section of New York State. Of this, 2.5 million acres are state-owned and are open to public hunting. This acreage provides a variety of hunting terrain that ranges from 100 feet above sea level to 46 mountains that tower to an elevation of 4000 feet or more. From wet lowlands and drainage basins to hardwood and softwood forests to rocky ridges, the landscape of the Adirondacks has it all. Approximately 80 percent of the Adirondacks are hardwood forest containing the wilderness whitetail's primary foods of beech, oak, and black cherry. Hemlock, spruce and fir are abundant and provide shelter and food for the deer herd's winter survival.

Deer numbers and food supplies are controlled by location. If the area is a designated "Forest Preserve" the timber is over 100 years old. This high canopy or "climax forest" setting has marginal ground vegetation for food. Managed timber properties on surrounding lands of vast acreages provide woodland vegetation at various stages of growth and deer food a-plenty.

THE CAMP TRADITION

As long as there have been deer and bear in the Adirondacks, there have been hunters and there have been camps. From Iroquois lodges to the bark shanties and lean-tos of the early frontiersmen to the permanent dwell-

For a three-day weekend every year these hunters have one thing in common: muzzleloading.

ings of late 1800s sportsmen, muzzleloading deer hunters have taken to the wilds like their "longhunter" ancestors. The grand daddy of all Adirondack hunting camps was Adirondack Lodge, built in 1878. The immense log structure was 105 feet long, 75 feet wide, and three stories tall. Today, most hunting camps are modest structures. But just the thought of being there conjures visions of a wisp of smoke coming out of the chimney, the camaraderie of fellow friends and hunters, and the welcome feel of a

Muzzleloader hunting is a deep-rooted tradition in the Adirondacks.

warm camp and hearty meal after a day of challenging the elements in the whitetail woods.

On the eve of this past season's hunt, I looked up to see my favorite constellation: Orion, the hunter. The geese, talking to one another on the small pond in front of the hunting cabin, completed the setting as the hunter's moon lit the still October woods. The hunters in the cabin carried on an eager conversation with the high hopes of bagging a deer or bear in the following days. This group, once again assembled in the camp, consisted of fathers, sons, brothers, and friends. No matter what walk of life we travel, for a three-day weekend every October we have one thing in common. Muzzleloading!

GUNS OF THE HUNTERS

New York State's big game muzzleloading season for whitetail deer and black bear requirements are "a gun loaded through the muzzle, having rifling in the barrel, and shooting a single projectile and having a minimum bore of .44 inch." As of 2002, scopes are legal on muzzleloaders. The guns used by the muzzleloader hunters in our camp are as diverse as the people themselves. Our members range from long-term devoted soot burners to novice muzzleloading enthusiasts with whitetails in mind. Mike Shafer is a devoted flintlock shooter with several Pennsylvania whitetails to his credit. He shoots a Thompson/Center Pennsylvania Hunter 50-cal. rifle. My brother Mark still shoots the early model 54-cal. T/C Renegade he bought new right after they came on the market in the late1970s. Jay Ritter hunted for two decades with a Thompson/Center Hawken, but these days he carries a 50-caliber bolt-action Remington 700 ML. My father has carried a variety of muzzleloaders over the years. This season he was using the .45 Winchester X-150 bolt-action.

John Ward is another member of the hunting party who shot a T/C Renegade with a drop-in Green Mountain round ball barrel. He enjoyed the rifle and he made meat with the rifle. But he now carries a 50-cal. Knight Wolverine with a synthetic stock and stainless steel barrel. Steve Santa-Maria bought a T/C Black Diamond rifle because of its safe, simple design, removable breech plug for easy straight-through cleaning, and synthetic stock for durability–but mostly because he wanted to participate in our camp's annual three day hunt.

The huge market that was spawned by the convenience offered by modern styled front-stuffers has introduced an entire new generation to muzzleloading. But one of the greatest things about muzzleloading is that you can enter the woods with a .45 sidehammer caplock or a .50 in-line bolt-action and have as much fun as anyone in the woods, and very possibly even more.

Each hunter has a different preference as to gun function and design.

Organization is essential for safety and success when conducting deer drives.

DRIVING FOR DEER

Our particular group had been hunting out of this camp for a decade. No matter what other seasons we hunt–be it bow or centerfire rifle–or what other tactics we employ–be it stand hunting, still-hunting, rattling, calling, or luring–on these special three-day muzzleloading hunts we do deer drives. Our camp is on timber company land. The mountainous terrain is sectioned off with logging roads, so driving the woodlots was a natural choice from day one. Each drive takes about 45 minutes to set up and 20 to 30 minutes to complete. It makes for a pleasantly brisk pace that melts a day away. The early season whitetails aren't into rut yet and are free-ranging to feed. North country deer cover a lot of ground. Some days you hit deer on half of the drives, and some days you never even see one.

Deer driving is somewhat of a misnomer as the deer, although intent on staying ahead of the intruders, use a wide variety of standard escape routes. Our five- to seven-man hunting party usually has two drivers and three watchers, or three drivers and four watchers. The watchers are set out usually in a "C" pattern, at 50 to 100 yard intervals, blocked from each other for safety's sake by terrain. Since coyotes are the chief tormentor, the drivers periodically bark and hoot to move deer and for two other important reasons. The first is so the drivers stay in line and perform the drive correctly. The second is so the watchers know the whereabouts of the drivers. Every drive has a set starting time and a set meeting place upon completion. If you are going to do drives, organization is imperative for safety and success.

Over the years our drives have produced success and surprise. I shot a 6-pointer once as I waited to start a drive. My brother Mark shot a buck as he approached his watch. Another time a stout black bear ran right up

A black bear rolling out of a deer drive can provide some exciting muzzleloader action.

to me at 30 feet, stood on its back feet and woofed at my motionless figure as it tried to wind me. Fishers, coyotes, bobcats, deer and bear have passed through our drives. An 8-pointer let me drive right up to it in a thicket of hemlocks before startling the bejeebers out of me. The biggest buck we ever had in a drive was a wide 10-pointer. Our flintlock hunter Mike Shafer had his sights on the buck but all that was showing was the head and antlers. The buck cut back through the drive right pass me. I could just see the rack as the buck broke skyline and made his escape over the mountain. Deer that move out ahead of the drivers present casual walking shots. The ones that wait to see what is driving them eventually bolt into flight and prove that a whitetail can run at 25 mph in cover and 40 mph in the open. Some years we get bucks, some years a bear, some years both, and some years nothing. And in the Adirondacks, that's why they call it hunting!

10

Active Times – Active Places

Mammalian biologists are just now beginning to appreciate the role that photoperiodism, the response of an animal to changes in the daily duration of sunshine, plays in a whitetail's life. Photoperiodism is primarily known for initiating the rut, but it actually governs a whitetail's life throughout the year. The increased daylight of the lengthening days of spring and the decreased light of the shortening days of autumn are transmitted to a whitetail's brain through its amazing eyes, which act as photoelectric cells. These cells in turn stimulate the pineal gland, part of the pituitary system of the brain, which synchronizes a whitetail's life through the seasons. The pineal gland controls the antler growth of spring and summer, the feeding frenzy of early autumn, the swollen neck and rampant testosterone of the rut, and the heavy winter coat and antler shedding of winter. Photoperiodism most notably controls a doe's life in autumn with the serge of estrogen that culminates in estrus and stimulates the rut. Leonard Lee Rue III describes photoperiodism, the response to light, in his book, *The Deer of North America*, thus: "Every step is orchestrated–a precise fitting together of season, conditions, and responses."

A SEASON OF CHANGE

After the mid summer sun begins to arch lower in the southern sky and the days gradually begin to shorten, whitetail-feeding activity starts to increase. Availability of ripening foods and the desire to eat are all part of the master plan. August, September, and October are big months for whitetails as they bulk up as much as 25% of their body weight for the rigors of mating season and ensuing winter. The increased consumption makes whitetails predictable and vulnerable due to their preoccupation with

Every step of the whitetail's life is orchestrated, a precise fitting together of season, conditions, and responses.

locating and obtaining food. Being crepuscular (active at dawn and dusk) by nature, sunup and sundown are peak hours of activity. In my region of the northeast, whitetails follow their nutritional instincts as the year progresses, eating their way first through leguminous foods such as alfalfa and clover, then corn, then apples, and then mast, the sustaining food throughout the fall and winter. Find the food of the moment and you have found the deer. Find the feeding does of November and you have found the bucks.

Do you know where your deer are? Mapping terrain will help you locate active habitat and travel corridors.

In the progression of autumn foods, acorns take center stage when they start hitting the ground. In the northeast, central, and southern regions of the United States, acorns are the number one whitetail food. In northern zones including the Adirondack Mountains where I hunt, acorns can compose 80% of the deer's diet. The deer not only move away from the seasonal foods and out of view, but they begin to eat, live, and sleep in close proximity to the acorn-bearing stands of oak. Nutritionally, the acorn is a highly desirable whitetail food, as it is high in fat and carbohydrates but easily digestible, allowing greater consumption, which itself increases protein intake. Simply put, nature allows the whitetail to consume greater quantities of acorns than any other food source. This consumption rapidly builds body reserves to sustain the deer through the winter months.

White oaks have leaves with rounded lobes and produce annual acorns that are the caviar of the acorn smorgasbord, so they're usually consumed first. Also, white acorns are less bitter as they contain less tannic acid than red acorns. Red oaks have leaves with pointed lobes and require two years to develop acorns. The red acorn is a hit-or-miss proposition, varying from a bumper crop one year to slim pickings the next.

LOCATING GAME

Do you know where your deer are? The only way to find out is get out there and look. And the best way to start is find the food source of the moment and work from there. I'm always amazed by the amount of hunters who hit the deer woods without an inkling of current deer activity. It's hard enough creating a rendezvous with known deer, let alone those whose habits are unknown to you. I recently heard someone say he saw deer eating apples under an old tree in October and that's where he was going hunting during the November season. Well, he ended up the only one at the apple tree. The apples were eaten in October and the deer moved on.

Not only will deer change feeding areas each autumn, they will change areas year to year. Two years ago I hunted a draw between two cornfields that was the definition of a staging area. A walnut tree and an old apple tree had dropped nuts and apples and lots of browse along the draw. There were rubs, scrapes, and trails along the length of the cover to the corn. One year later there were no walnuts, no apples, and no deer.

Coming from a region of .6 bucks per square mile and wilderness blocks 20 miles square, I carry a topographic map, compass, and binoculars and I walk miles of deer trails to locate the preferred foods of autumn. Edge covers with good browse surrounding an abundant acorn crop are my preferred location. The harder the weather conditions of the approaching winter, the harder the deer will feed. Deer movement isn't always defined by clear-cut tracks, so rubs, scrapes, beds, and fresh droppings will be my guide. Tracks made on successive days are often hard to evaluate under stable weather conditions.

When I locate an active area, I then concentrate on the access trails leading from bedding areas. These are dictated by the advantage of terrain for view, air current, or protection from the weather. The need to feed and the need to breed are what keep whitetails moving. It is up to you to interpret the conditions at hand and find the deer.

Having hunted whitetails in the Midwest on several occasions, I've found that binoculars play a huge part in scouting. As I once learned on a sheep hunt, you can cover a lot more ground with your eyes than with your legs. Topographical maps from the United States Geological Survey Information Services (1-800-USA-MAPS) have always provided hunters with a feel for the terrain. Aerial photos can provide you with a bird's-eye view of the cover, identifying likely deer habitat, foods, and foliage as well as mountain benches and farm country funnels. These can be ordered from Aerial Photography Field Office, User Services, at (801) 975-3503.

Just last year I discovered myTopo.com, a product of Beartooth Mapping, Inc., (877) 587-9004. For $14.95 they will center a map anywhere in the United States, printed with precise navigational grids that are perfect for compass and GPS use. These customized maps are large

Still-hunters need to eliminate and control as much of their human scent as possible.

This hunter is using a scented decoy and a deer call to lure deer in. Always wear a safety harness when using a treestand.

Few hunting thrills rival a buck responding to antler rattling.

format, 24"x36", and are waterproof and tear-resistant. myTopo.com's maps are even personalized with map title and your name. You can build one over the internet or they will build you one by phone. These are a great scouting and hunting companion in big country.

CREATING OPPORTUNITIES

It is said that the whitetail deer's sense of smell is 100 times more acute than that of a human. Deer know each other's scent. Deer scent marks boundaries, and it marks the trails they follow. A buck's scent proclaims his presence during the mating season and a doe's scent initiates the mating season. But I have noticed that air current is one of the least understood phases of deer hunting. More hunters tip off more deer with human scent than all other blunders combined. A deer's nose is always in search of a scent pattern, either welcome or unwelcome, as it moves through the woods. Deer, especially prowling bucks, never commit to any opening until they are certain there is no apparent danger.

I do a lot of still-hunting along deer trails during the Adirondack muzzleloader hunt in mid-October. As a primitive hunter, you need to create an enticing atmosphere that won't repel a whitetail. To start with you need to eliminate and control as much of your human scent as possible. This starts at home with a clean body and clothing washed with unscented detergents. Since I live in a rural setting, my clothing is then hung in a screened porch and air washed. However you achieve it, scent must

be kept at a minimum for close encounters with deer. In recent years I have been using human odor eliminators from Pete Rickard's, Inc. (800-282-5663), the original scent manufacturer.

The one smell that is most overlooked by muzzleloader hunters is inherent to our sport: muzzleloaders themselves. Rickard's also is the distributor for Crouse's masking scents for guns. In either pine or cedar, these scented gun oils and bore cleaners have worked extremely well for both gun cleaning, and scent masking of my muzzleloaders.

When using a ground blind or treestand, location and comfort are everything. The location should be the product of your scouting in a currently active deer area with multiple trails. Deer stands should facilitate easy-in, easy-out with little disturbance. You do not want to over-advertise your presence. Do your best to determine the air current during the time of day you will be hunting. Then set your stand 25 to 50 yards upwind of your selected site. Get comfortable. Most of us can't sit still in the comfort of our home for two hours, let alone in the woods. Be sure to cut shooting lanes, but not clear-cut your stand surroundings. Sitting in the wide open and fidgeting is no way to entice deer. An excellent tool for trimming selective shooting lanes is Gerber's Deluxe Hunter's Pruning Kit. This compact ratchet pruner and sliding saw worked great for trimming branches along a trails and cutting tree limbs.

Whitetails communicate, vocally and by their scent, and visually confirm every move they make. The use of

Scent, although its strongest asset, can be a whitetail's downfall. This buck has fallen for Trail's End scent dispensed by The Ultimate Scrape-Dripper from Wildlife Research Center.

Trail cameras don't guarantee a trophy, but they can definitely enhance the anticipation of the hunt.

deer calls at the appropriate time can be very effective. From the pre-rut calm to the peak rut frenzy, the right call at the right time will produce a response from deer. Softly breathing into a grunt tube, much as though you were fogging a pane of glass, creates the universal communicating and calming call. A little stronger call will produce the content grunt, another sound made by bucks and does. The distress bleats of a fawn can stir up the pot. But if the bucks are rutting strong, choppy grunts can instigate action in a hurry from scrape-checking bucks and other curious deer. Sitting on a super-fresh scrape, I once called in two bucks at once using these loud guttural sounds. The True Talker deer call from Hunter Specialties (800-728-0321) can produce all 13 sounds in a whitetail vocabulary.

Scent, although a deer's strongest asset, can be his downfall. Following the seasonal flow of deer activity will dictate how you call and use scent. Wildlife Research Center (800-873-5873) offers a complete line of scent elimination products, cover scents, and deer scents and lures. Early season scents to entice deer include food/cover scents and non-sexual urine scents. Pre-rut is a good time for buck scents to agitate testosterone-charged competitors. Estrous doe scent is very productive during peak rut. Whether set out in scent canisters, dragged on a trail rag, worn on your person, or doctoring a scrape, lure works at the appropriate time. When you add the sound of rattling antlers to lure in the air, you can create a real enticer.

One of the most exciting events in deer hunting is rattling in a rut-charged buck. Of the half dozen I have rattled in while muzzleloading, one stands out: an Illinois buck that tore up turf, thrashed trees, and charged every moving thing in route to my stand location. That buck would have been an excellent candidate for a decoy. Decoys in buck or doe form, doctored with scent, can also entice deer throughout the seasonal and physical changes of autumn. Decoys can have a calming effect on approaching deer. Or they can drive a territorial buck right off the deep end. A word of caution: use decoys only in a private or otherwise safe hunting area. Someone else's mistaken shot at the decoy could easily find you instead.

ANTICIPATION

The anticipation of the hunt is what drives us. A scouting aid used by many hunters today is the trail camera. Once you find an active deer area, a trail camera set in a strategic location can take photos of the passing deer. Every roll of film has something new. Photos range from wild turkeys, to red and gray foxes, to coyotes, to many does and yearlings, and several nice bucks. The nicest buck that ever passed my camera made but one appearance, never to be seen again. Time and date printed on each picture allow you to pattern the resident game's habits. Trail cameras don't guarantee a trophy, but the photos can definitely enhance the anticipation of the hunt. I now use the camera all year 'round, concentrating on predators in winter and whitetails the rest of the year.

DRIVING FORCE

The moon has long been credited with affecting man and animal alike. There are two prominent theories concerning the effect of the moon on deer. One is based on the phases of the autumn moon and the response of an animal to changes in day length (photoperiodism). Charles J. Alsheimer's book *Hunting Whitetails by the Moon* contains significant evidence to tie the breeding season and the autumn moon phases together. The October full moon starts the rut by initiating buck scraping and the initial estrus cycle of does. The next full moon, combined with the rapidly decreasing daylight, kicks off the breeding phase, with peak breeding beginning 10 days after the hunter's moon. Jeff Murray, in his book *Moonstruck*, explains the position of the moon in relationship to peak hours of whitetail activity. The moon has an elliptical or flattened-circle orbit, so twice a day it is closer to the earth than during the rest of its orbit. As Murray puts it, "overhead and under foot." These two periods of moon orbit are the peak periods of whitetail activity. The most intense effect in activity is when the moon is directly overhead.

11
Walking & Stalking

Not every lone hunter was meant to be still, i.e., hunting from a ground blind or a treestand. As advantageous as a well-scouted, well-placed stand location can be, not every hunter can sit still. Not every hunter wants to sit still. I cut my teeth on cruising deer trails for whitetails. It doesn't take long to learn the first mistake is moving too fast. I learned that my best luck still-hunting, one step at a time through woodland covers, was at the first hours of morning and the last hours of the day when deer were moving. If hunting in a snowstorm I headed for the bedding areas. Still-hunting in forested lands usually produces shots at unknowing deer, or glimpses of a bounding, escaping deer. Quiet clothing and soft-soled shoes for silent passage; compact binoculars for spotting eyes, ears, legs and antlers in dense cover; a deer call or turkey call to cover your sounds; an open-sighted rifle–all of these are standard equipment for slipping through the edges of an Adirondack hemlock swamp or spotting a blowdown-bedded whitetail during a late season Pennsylvania snowstorm. Close-quarters still-hunting is a great way to get to know the game you pursue and the country you hunt. But in big mountain country, or the vastness of the high plains or tundra, you need to cover more ground as not all game hugs the cover or has cover to hug. And you can cover a lot more ground with a good pair of binoculars from a vantage point than you ever will with your legs. Walking and stalking is an exciting and invigorating way to hunt the big game of North America.

WEANED ON WOODCHUCKS

Late spring and early summer Sunday afternoons meant woodchuck hunting with my dad in the mid-1960s. It was a wonderful time in both our lives and my introduction to hunting as a kid. And what a positive

Although productive, hunting from ground blinds and treestands is not favored by all hunters.

You will cover a lot more ground with your eyes than you ever will with your legs in big country.

introduction it was. The lush, green, rolling farm pastures evoke fond memories to this day as I remember walking the countryside, glassing for game, stalking into .22 range, and making the best of each shell that my father handed to me, one at a time.

Woodchuck hunting in the 1960s was a very popular and accepted springtime recreation. Due to this popularity, the woodchuck in turn made immeasurable contributions toward the development of sophisticated, flat-shooting modern rifle calibers and appropriate shooting gear. Whether called woodchuck, groundhog or whistle-pig, these varmints are taken at great distances with modern rifles, 400 yards being not uncommon. Trying to get close for a shot with my first muzzleloader, a 45-caliber Thompson/Center Seneca I bought in the mid '70s, showed me that woodchucks are worthy game for the primitive hunter. And great practice for hunting bigger game animals.

Glassing them from a distance was the easy part. Stalking within 100 yards or less was the challenge. Since the woodchuck is found in and along forest and farming country throughout the eastern half of the United States, there is a lot of boundary cover to work with. Fencerows, woodlot edges and rolling-meadows contain more woodchuck holes than you think, once you actively begin to seek them out. Strategically planning your move using the available cover becomes the name of the game.

My best day ever was three chucks for five shots with that little percussion rifle. In the 1990s my father and I again found ourselves enjoying this spring hunting ritual with Simmons- or Bushnell-scoped flat shooting muzzleloading rifles such as the 50-caliber Remington 700ML shooting a Remington 289-gr. copper bullet, and the 45-caliber Knight DISC Rifle shooting the 180-grain all-

Woodchucks are worthy game for practicing your walking, stalking and shooting skills.

copper Barnes Expander MZ. Shooting 100 and 150-grain loads of Pyrodex Pellets allowed these rifles to effectively take woodchucks at ranges exceeding 150 yards.

BLACKPOWDER ABOVE THE TREELINE

A mature bull caribou with his white neck, gray-brown body and towering palmated antlers is one of the handsomest big game animals in North America. The four primary sub-species of Mountain, Barren Ground, Quebec-Labrador, and Woodland stretch geographically from Alaska to Newfoundland. Although each species' bull possesses similar antler formations typical of the caribou family, the differences in the shovel over the snout, the palmated bez strutting forward off each antler above the head, and the sweeping beams and tine length are obvious once you become a student of these roving members of the deer family.

Slipping along game trails while carefully scanning your surroundings is an educational, enjoyable and rewarding way to muzzleloader hunt.

Longer shots are the norm when walking and stalking in big country. Good optics, a flat-shooting rifle with a range-proven load and a steady shooting rest such as this Stoney Point Hike n' Hunt shooting stick are essential.

Caribou country is often barren, moss- and lichen-covered landscape strewn with time-ravaged rocks on the flats and ridges, with scrub spruce bottoms and bogs between the heights of ground. One of my first images of bull caribou came in northern Quebec in 1981 while I was glassing the terrain from a freighter canoe. Peering through my binoculars, I saw three nice bulls on the skyline with their noses pressed to the ground. My guide quickly pointed out that they weren't feeding. They were pressing their noses to the ground to keep the ever-annoying flies out of their nostrils.

Caribou was the first big game I ever traveled to hunt. I thought woodchucks were tough to get close to with my 45-caliber half-stock until I tried getting within 100 yards of a perpetually moving caribou across endless tundra! Glassing and spotting bulls on distant ridges, beaching the canoe, and heading up the mountains gave me an education in walking and stalking like I had never experienced. After one such stalk, my father, the Inuit Indian guide Raymond, and I turned to see another bull passing below several hundred yards away. The bull was headed for the saddle at the end of the mountain. The bull disappeared around the mountainside and in a flash I was off to the races in an attempt to head this caribou off at the pass.

I reached the saddle, peeked over the rise, and there was the bull. I lay prone and tried to calm my breathing. When the wind isn't blowing, there is a deafening silence on the tundra. I paused a breath, squeezed the trigger, and audibly heard the whack of that 130-grain patched round ball. The handsome bull was my first "big game" with a muzzleloader. I have hunted caribou on three occasions

This magnificent Central Barren Ground Caribou was taken by Brian Dam near Courageous Lake in the Northwest Territories and ranks #4 in the Longhunter Muzzleloading Big Game Record Book.

and filled my tag on two. On my third hunt I wanted "big." I spotted a bull against skyline two ridges away. After further inspection with binoculars my guide Elias exclaimed, "He is at least 60 inches across. If we can get that one you better go home happy." The bull disappeared like a ghost. But I will never forget his majestic image against the tundra sky.

HIGH PLAINS ANTELOPE

The unique pronghorn antelope has existed here in America, near to its present form, for 20 million years. It is a far more ancient inhabitant than our bison or elk. Several factors may have contributed to its longevity. Large eyes placed high on the side of the pronghorn's head give it wide range, eight-power vision. An enlarged heart, lungs and windpipe not only let it maintain speed for long distance runs but make it the fastest animal on the entire continent. Some interestingly peculiar things about this animal are that it has hooves without dewclaws like a giraffe. It has four stomachs and a gall bladder like a goat, and it sheds its horns, which is something unique in the animal world.

Even the pronghorn's alarm system is unique. The whitetail deer flags its tail when alarmed, but the pronghorn flashes its whole rump by making the white hair stand on end. One last feature of note to hunters is the bone strength of the pronghorn. Tests have shown that it takes 45,300 lbs. per square inch to crush a pronghorn

The truly unique sagebrush country pronghorn will test a muzzleloader hunter's walking and stalking skills. Photo: Debra Bradbury.

Rancher Mike Henry, the author, and noted gunsmith Dale Storey with a Wyoming pronghorn buck taken with a 50-cal. double-barrel Kodiak Rifle.

RANGEFINDERS

In big country, range estimation can pose a problem. It doesn't matter whether you are shooting a flintlock rifle with blackpowder and a patched round ball, or a scoped modern in-line loaded with 150-gr. of Pyrodex Pellets and a sabot bullet. Both guns have their effective range limits. Rangefinders such as the compact, handheld Bushnell Yardage Pro Scout are easy to pack and solve the question of range estimation from 10 to 700 yards.

The newest generation of hunting optics features laser rangefinder/binocular combinations that are truly suited for hunting big game in big country. The 8x36 Bushnell Yardage Pro Quest enables the hunter to spot game and determine range simultaneously from 15 to 1300 yards. This unit helps the hunter select landmarks and vantage points that will place him within the effective shooting range of his muzzleloader.

leg bone. To put this in perspective, their bone strength is eight times stronger than that of a beef steer.

Hunting pronghorn on the western plains is the closest thing to going to Africa as you can do in North America. Hunting pronghorn is both fun and affordable, and it's an excellent choice for hunters testing the waters of the guided hunting experience. Although Arizona and New Mexico's pronghorns rule the top spots in the Longhunter Muzzleloading Big Game Record Book, Wyoming is the number one pronghorn state by population, producing quality 13- to 16-inch horns up to 80-inch class bucks.

The sheer number of game is the most thrilling thing about hunting the high plains. Pronghorn, mule deer, elk and river bottom whitetails can be seen as you glass the endless draws and buttresses landscaped with sagebrush, yucca and prickly pear cactus and river bottoms lined with cottonwood trees. Driving to destinations, glassing, walking and checking every cut and draw for game is how you hunt pronghorn and the easiest way to get close for a shot with muzzleloading firearms. Spotting pronghorns on the plains and stalking into range presents its own set of challenges. If you see them, chances are they see you. I have been stuck by cactus and greeted by rattlesnakes and have taken two nice pronghorn bucks. Good walking shoes, good optics, a range finder, and a well sighted-in rifle are highly recommended for hunting pronghorns.

A BIG MUZZLELOADING MULIE

The mule deer inhabits the deserts, prairies and mountains of our western states. A large-racked mule deer, like trophy class members of all the deer family, is something to appreciate. Adult mule deer bucks do carry well-formed racks at earlier age than whitetails. This explains why many eastern hunters are awed by the first adult mule deer buck they lay there eyes on. Unlike the whitetail's antlers consisting of a main beam with singular perpendicular tines, the mule deer's antlers divide into two main beams with each forking into tines. This type

THE OPTICAL ADVANTAGE

Experience is the best teacher. On my first pronghorn hunt in 1983 I discovered the difference between good binoculars and bad.

Glassing the expansive landscape for hours on end was exhausting with an inexpensive pair of field glasses that proved to be not much more than a pair of spent toilet paper tubes with glass in each end. The result was piercing eye-strain headaches. The meaning of such terms as "magnification," "brightness," "resolution" and "field-of-view" became glaringly obvious as my envious eyeballs gazed through the clarity of my guide's quality 10x42 binoculars.

I returned home on a mission to find a pair of binoculars that suited my hunting needs. Since whitetails constitute the bulk of my hunting, I looked for binoculars that featured moderate magnification and chose a pair of Bausch and Lomb Custom Compact 7x26. These binoculars are now almost paint-bare from two decades of serious use.

For big country, my eyes are much happier with a pair of Bushnell 10x42. The best way to select the best optics is to go to a store and look through a variety of binoculars and see what works best for you. A pair of 7x binoculars with excellent resolution is more useful than a pair of 10x with poor resolution. And remember, when hunting with binoculars, let the optics work for you. Take a solid rest: sitting with your elbows on your knees, leaning against a tree or over a bolder or holding the binoculars against your upright gun barrel while kneeling. The steadier your optics, the less eye fatigue for you and the higher the chances of spotting that big buck's antlers sticking above the brush in a distant draw.

Ron Hansen poses with his incredible Colorado mule deer buck.

The nocturnal Wyoming river bottom buck with Russian olive bark crammed in his antler bases.

of antler growth is called bifurcated. Mule deer have large ears and as one would expect have excellent hearing. They also have great vision. But like whitetails, mule deer possess a highly developed sense of smell. I have hunted mountain mule deer in the Colorado Rockies and prairie mule deer on the high plains of Wyoming. They may live in geographically different locations, but they detect danger and use the terrain, each to their advantage. Ironically, the biggest mountain mule deer I ever encountered was while big horn sheep hunting in the La Garita Mountains in southern Colorado in 1993. Just above a treeline at 13,000 feet, my guide and I spotted two twin mind-boggling 4x4 bucks as we approached our targeted rams. My best mule deer buck was a modest 4x4 I shot in Wyoming with a patched round ball fired from my full-stock 54-caliber custom rifle.

One of the finest mule deer bucks I have written about was taken by former Grand Junction, Colo., resident Ron Hansen. Ron hunted for years with a 50-caliber CVA Mountain Rifle that he had built from a kit. Ron had taken three mule deer bucks with that rifle during the September Colorado muzzleloader mule deer seasons. Ron's favored tactic was to cruise mountainside mule deer trails under the autumn canopy of golden aspens and then take stands at active trail crossings.

On one particular afternoon Ron had waited for his son Chris to get home from school. A 3:00 p.m. departure allowed just a couple hours of hunting light. Hunting time even became shorter when Ron's first choice hunting spot was inaccessible. Finally getting parked at another

hunting spot, Chris followed his dad along a trail to a favorite watch of Ron's. For the next hour a mule deer doe and yearling entertained father and son. As the sun lowered, so did the temperature of the crisp mountain air. Chris' chattering teeth became audible. Ron decided to get moving and hunt the trail back to the truck. About halfway back up the mountain trail Ron spotted movement, freezing himself and Chris in their tracks. What Ron Hansen saw in the fading afternoon sun was a sight hunters' dreams are made of: a bachelor band of five big mule deer bucks.

The fourth buck in line was the biggest. Ron dropped the hammer as they passed in single file at 15 yards. A 5x5 with a 32-inch spread and over 180 inches of antler made for a very memorable afterschool mulie for the Hansens.

WHITETAILS IN REVERSE

In the foothill and mountain country where I live in the Adirondack Mountains, the forested lands are the high country with fertile valleys below. In wide-open Wyoming, the high plains are a broken, barren land with the river bottoms home to the trees and fertile grasses. And that is where the whitetails call home, where the cover is. The river bottoms have water, food and shelter. The pronghorn antelope cruise the edges of the bottoms, the mule deer spend time there, but the whitetails live there, under the upper canopy of cottonwoods and within the extensive Russian olive trees. Seeking them out as they would beech whips or an alder swamp back east, these Wyoming whitetails use the Russian olive trees to rub on, scrape under, feed upon, bed within, and travel within. As I would soon find out, spotting whitetails before they spot you in this cover presents its own set of challenges. When you are down in the river bottoms you can see under the trees' canopy. But from the bordering high ground, the dense foliage hides the deer well. Spot and stalking, taking a stand along an open bottom, and walking off long stretches of river bed toward a posted hunter are the tactics that work best on these river bottom bucks.

During one memorable hunt several years ago, the rancher who was my host spoke of a drop-tine buck that had gone nocturnal with the onset of the November rut. On the third evening of the hunt my guide and I circled the high ground to glass the distant bottom for approaching deer.

Sure enough, way down in the riverbed was the 10-point buck with two 6-inch drop tines feeding on Russian olives and working his way in our direction. With the sun setting, we headed to an ambush site at the narrows of the riverbed in an old cottonwood blowdown.

It was a pleasantly nervous wait knowing there was an amazing buck moving our way. Garrett, my guide, looked through the horizontal tree trunks at sunset and calmly whispered, "The buck is walking right by us. I mean right here." I looked over the barrel, lined up the sights, and cocked the hammer. The cottonwood's root base blocked my view as I intently watched the bottom. The handsome whitetail walked through my sights at 20 yards as I dropped the hammer on the 50-cal. caplock.

HUGE BLACK BEAR

The black bear is generally thought of as the smallest of the North American bears. The Adirondack region in upstate New York contains a healthy population of black bears holding around 4000 of the state's 6000 bears. A 300- to 400-lb. male is considered a large adult black bear. New York State currently has 27 black bears on record weighing in at over 500 lbs.

Black bears are opportunists when it comes to food and habitat. With a range of 5 to 15 miles, black bears are at home in all of the two million acres of public hunting grounds in the Adirondack region. The black bear has provided thrills for countless hunters over the years because of its adaptability to modern civilization. But the big bears that live the longest generally live in the deep woods. The largest Adirondack bear to date had a dressed weight of 660 pounds; New York State's Department of Environmental Conservation estimated the live weight to be a whopping 746 pounds.

For big bears, the good old days are right now. All but two of the 27 bears heavier than 500 pounds have been taken since 1980. Twelve of these bruins have been taken since 1990. New York State's special muzzleloader deer/bear season in the northern Adirondack Mountain region in mid-October is an excellent opportunity for the muzzle-

Bill Wharton with the incredibly large hide of his 581-pound black bear that measured 6 feet wide by 7 feet 7 inches long.

loader hunter who has a bear in mind. Most Adirondack black bears are taken during chance encounters while whitetail hunting. New York State's #1 muzzleloader bear by weight was taken in just this manner.

Bill Wharton is a charter member of the New York States Outdoor Guides Association that was formed in 1973. He has guided many successful Adirondack whitetail and black bear hunters over the last 30 years. By the last day of the 7-day muzzleloader hunt his clients had filled tags and returned home. Bill took the opportunity to invite his cousin Dave Davis along for a day's outing with their smokepoles. As afternoon arrived, the two hunters found themselves approaching an area where Bill had discovered a large bear den six years earlier. It was a classic bear den under the root ball of a large tree. Wharton had curiously checked the den each year but never had seen any activity. Now, in the middle of October, he didn't expect to see any this visit either.

The first thing that caught the experienced guide's eye was the chewed-off softwoods and beech tops around the area. Fresh bear tracks headed in the direction of the den. Bill collected his hunting partner and they planned their approach. The muzzleloader hunters eased towards the root ball fortress. What happened next happened quickly

NAVIGATION TOOLS

Getting there and back again has always been a concern to hunters entering new territory. Hunting large wilderness tracts such as those of the Adirondacks or northern Maine, the vastness of open tundra, or the humbling size of the Rocky Mountains makes you curious to know exactly where you are amidst such immense topography. A topographical map of the region in my pocket and a pin-on bubble compass that I can glance at for quick reference have always served me well.

I have been fortunate to be able to improve my ability by hunting with people like my friend John Ward, who possesses superior natural navigational skills. It is one thing to navigate on a clear day when landmarks are visible. It is another to find your way in dense fog and rain or a white-out snowstorm. Global Positioning System (GPS) units that are networked with global positioning satellites have been used for the navigation of watercraft for many years. During the last decade they have become widely used by hunters to mark locations of game activity while scouting, to find their way in and out of unexplored hunting grounds, and to mark downed game for a return trip with the pack horses in the morning.

GPS is a wonderful tool. But in mountainous terrain or on a cloudy day, you will be glad you still have a USGS topographic map and a compass. Having hunted elk, mule deer, and bighorn at eleva-

tions ranging from 7,000 to 14,000 feet, I find that an altimeter is handy for locating camp in a storm or after nightfall. Nothing is more exhausting after a full day of hunting than missing camp coming off the mountain and having to climb back up to find it!

Photo: Jeff Davis

and prompted an adrenaline rush that both hunters will long remember.

A large bear suddenly emerged from the den. Wharton took the bruin behind the shoulder with the first round ball. As Bill backed away to reload he looked up. The big bear had returned to action, snarling and popping his teeth. Davis took aim and fired. His shot went right into the open mouth of the bear. As the bruin went down, Bill got another shot in for safekeeping. The rattled hunters knew they had almost bitten off more than they could chew. The huge, 20+-year-old black bear had a dressed weight of 581 pounds and estimated live weight of 657 pounds, according to the NYSDEC bear unit's formula. The bear's unfleshed hide measured an incredible 6 feet by 7 feet, 7 inches. The big bruin's skull measured 20-1/2 inches.

Not bad for an "abandoned" den!

12

Muzzleloading Satellites

*T*hree different toms in three different trees with three different harems began to spontaneously gobble back and forth as the sun peeked over the horizon. After a half hour of exchanges to hen calls, all three gobblers dropped off their roosts and headed over the hill with their hens. Within moments of their departure I heard movement to my left. My muzzleloading shotgun was raised and ready, when a lone, silent tom stuck his head out of the thicket.

Fresh tracks! The three does were walking together. The long-stride, wide-haunch buck walked off to the side. Soon, I noticed another track shadowing the big buck and the does. I hadn't tracked very far in the new snow when I heard grunting and breaking limbs. Suddenly, a 4-point buck was running directly down the barrel of my rifle.

The big bull elk in the basin below was working overtime trying to keep his cows in order. Easing through the timber, I began picking out three bulls that were moving through the golden aspens as they circled the bull and his harem. The calling of the herd bull had them all worked up as each began raking spruce trees with his antlers. A 4x4 bull never knew I was there until my .54 percussion rifle roared.

The 50-inch bull moose wasn't quite comfortable with our calls and our presence and disappeared into the Maine woods. My hunting partner and I sat tight and continued to call in the direction of the cow and calf before us. The two moose suddenly looked behind them. A 40-inch bull with tall, thin palms was cutting in on the rutting action, pounding right into the crosshairs of my scoped in-line rifle.

Just because satellites live in the shadows of the dominant males, as does this timber-hugging herd bull, that doesn't mean they're inferior game.

SATELLITES?

Turkeys, whitetails, elk, or moose need not be dominant males to attract the interest of the muzzleloader hunter. During mating season, younger, older, or less aggressive males of the species are pushed out of the breeding picture as dominant males take their place in the social order. This doesn't mean that the subordinate males don't want a part of the mating picture; quite the contrary. They will spend the entire period of their mating season on the periphery of the social center of the in-season females and dominant males. Thus these gobblers, bucks, and bulls have become known as satellites. Not risking aggressive advances by dominant males, satellites are forced to the outskirts, where they constantly orbit, to observe the behavior of their superiors. Although the dominant males have earned an established rank, their work is never-ending as the satellites are always lurking in the thickets, waiting to jump at the opportunity to mate with an unattended female.

The turkey episode described above was a perfect example of the silent approach as the tom waited for the boss gobblers to leave with their flocks before he made his move on the unattended, lonely hen of our calls. The 4-point buck was shadowing and observing the superior whitetail and the three does until he observed just a little too closely. That's when the bigger buck chased him right back to me. The three bull elk were just frustrated at being no match for the herd bull. All they could do was bugle in vain and shred trees. The smart bull moose sensed trouble and took flight. The satellite bull jumped at the chance to court the cows, not knowing that his fate would be determined by the squeeze of a trigger.

Concentrating on orbiting competitors will increase your muzzleloader hunting action.

HUNTING PRIMITIVE SATELLITES

Several factors contribute to becoming successful on satellites. Being opportunists who quietly watch, listen, scent, and wait for a careless moment, satellites stay secluded in the best available cover near the center of activity as they defensively sneak around the peripheral edges of the territory of the boss males. This most often produces close-quarters, fast-action hunting. Your muzzleloading shotgun or rifle should be loaded with a proven load in the hands of a prepared shooter.

Finding their geographical social center is the biggest step in locating your game during mating season. Turkeys have dusting grounds, whitetails have scrapes, elk have wallows, and moose thrash saplings, shrubs, and trees near their bedding areas. But your best bet is to find the females: that's where the males will be. By working with the wind

Pay attention! Calling can produce surprising results.

to keep your scent out of the area and carefully slipping into the social areas, not marching right in, you can keep the critters at ease. Turkey roosts are a great example. You can literally see your chances fly away when you stumble upon roosting birds. The deer family will also flee, because not only can they see and hear you coming, they can smell you, too. But once you have achieved position within the boundaries of the mating game, you can find some of the best muzzleloader hunting action available. And you don't always have to call to be successful. Still-hunting, or drifting towards game to put yourself in their line of travel, can put you in position to set up for a shot.

The basics of close quarters hunting definitely applies when muzzleloading for satellites:

1) Your clothing must match your background.

2) Cover your hands and face as these parts show movement the most.

3) Boots with dark soles are a must for ground hunting.

4) Avoid direct sunlight. Position yourself to face west in morning and east in the afternoon.

5) Think about your intentions when you pick a spot to sit down or set a tree stand. Inside of 40 yards you should concentrate on blending in; outside of 40 yards you should concentrate on breaking up your outline.

6) Use either a cover scent or lure to match the game hunted. Your clothing should be air-cleaned or scent-washed to eliminate any human or foreign odors.

Remember, these peripheral or satellite toms, bucks, or bulls are all outsiders. They were either too small or less aggressive or have recently lost their position of dominance to a former satellite, who is now in his prime and top dog. Satellites can range in age from young, frisky jakes, spike horns and rag horns to old long beards and impressively antlered bucks and bulls. Hunting satellites greatly expands your primitive hunting horizons. And since peak activity for satellites is during the mating season of each, calling is a most effective method to bring these orbiters into muzzleloading range. Satellites all want desperately what they can't have, if only to get a glimpse of the status once theirs.

Basic calls for each should include the following:

Turkey - A turkey hunter should be able to give a yelp, a content cluck and putt, a purr, and a cutt. He should be conversant in basic turkey talk using box calls, mouth diaphragm, peg and slate, or wing bone call in combination with decoys. One or two hen decoys can be a real clincher for satellite toms.

Whitetail - The deer hunter should be able to produce a fawn bleat, a soft doe call (the universal deer call created by breathing into your grunt tube as though you're fogging a pane of glass), a grunt, and the short, loud and abrupt tending buck call. Horn rattling is another effective method. Rattling and calling produce a mix of responders that can range from a dominant buck showing up, to defend his turf, to a challenging buck, to a satellite buck.

Elk - An elk hunter should be able to create various bull calls using a diaphragm much like a turkey call (for loud challenges and deep, guttural grunting) and a bugling tube (for tone and distance). The cow call is used to complete the bull/cow scenario to challenge bulls or entice frustrated orbiting bulls.

Moose - Cow moose notify bulls by calling out with a "*meaauugh...meaauugh.*" Bulls in earshot respond with primal grunts and bellows of "*ugghh...ugghh*" as they move toward the cow's position. Some callers still use the handmade birchbark call. Many cup their hands over their mouth, pressing their nose shut with their forefingers, to produce an effective call. Thrashing saplings, shrubs or trees with a stick while calling is also effective. Mating moose are extremely susceptible to calling and can cover a great deal of ground in a hurry.

SATELLITE CALLING = MUZZLELOADING ACTION

Turkeys – After trying several types of turkey calls I stopped on a plateau and tried my box call. The volume of the call stirred a distant bird. I responded to the gobbler with rapid cuts at first, then some mild clucks and soft yelping as the session progressed. When the bird got close, I nudged him into shooting range using soft purring. The big tom finally appeared, took one look at a pair of hen decoys, and charged right into muzzleloading shotgun range. The lone, satellite tom weighed 21 lbs. and had a 9-inch beard and 1-inch spurs.

Whitetails – On a rainy November day I headed up a trail to a location where there is an annual scrape. Every year it is the neighborhood guest book. I arrived at the scrape site to find it had been freshly worked. All

Close-quarters muzzleloader hunting for bugling bull elk is truly exciting.

Many moose hunters still use a handmade birch bark call to produce the mating sound of the bull.

David King took this Maine moose with a Thompson/Center Black Diamond .50 rifle shooting three 50-grain Pyrodex Pellets behind a 300-gr. 44-caliber XTP bullet in a Magnum Express Sabot.

the way to the scrape I had been laying a scent line with droplets of buck lure. I concealed myself in a blowdown about 30 yards up the trail before starting to call with a grunt tube using the *burp-burp-burp tending* grunt. In less than 10 minutes, I heard a deer trotting and jumping over obstacles as it approached. With my rifle raised and ready, I glanced back over my shoulder toward the scrape. There stood a spike horn that was looking past me at the other buck. The approaching deer stopped just outside a shooting lane. Then the spike horn standing in the scrape made me. He bolted, the other buck bolted, and I sat there in disbelief at what had just happened.

Elk – A bull suddenly bugled not a hundred yards away in the heavy timber. Simultaneously, two curious cow elk came up the game trail. For several minutes, cows and hunters stood in a frozen standoff. The lead cow finally bolted and the other one followed. Just as Don Robbins and his guide were thinking they had blown it,

the Colorado bull bugled within 75 yards. The hunters quickly moved to an area of more open timber ahead. They could hear the bull walking in a thick stand of lodgepole pines. The elk let rip with another bugle. The guide did some soft cow calling. That was all it took. Heavy breathing and a determined stride could be heard. Then antlers appeared, bobbing above the scrub pines. The big elk stepped right into a perfectly clear shooting lane where Robbins dropped the bull with a 430-grain lead slug fired from a .54 full-stock percussion rifle.

Moose – David "Dirt" King was enjoying his Maine moose hunt, having drawn one of the coveted non-resident permits. He was amazed at the size of a bull he had seen. It had a 60-plus inch spread and resembled a Clydesdale with antlers. But the bull was wise, not responding to calling but concentrating on gathering cows. Another bull appeared in the area. On closer inspection, the orbiting bull just kept staying in the shadows, cruising the boss bull's turf. While David's hunting partner continued calling to keep the bull's attention, King put himself in position to intercept the moving satellite. A 150-grain powder charge and a sabot bullet dropped the bull in its tracks. The moose had heavy beams, deep dishes, and long points. It weighed more than 1200 lbs. and rendered 400 lbs. of meat.

CONCLUSION

I'll take any satellite that responds to calling. Just because he isn't the dominant male doesn't mean he makes for a lesser-quality hunting experience. There are many more satellite gobblers, bucks, and bulls than there are dominant trophy-class ones. You can choose to hunt either one. Hunting the perimeters of mating season social centers is challenging and fun. It requires the basics of close-quarters hunting and a calling strategy to match the situation at hand. If you are interested in having more game to hunt, stop focusing just on Mr. Big and get into the orbiting zone for muzzleloading satellites. You just might be surprised at the result.

13

Tale Of The True Talker

It is no accident that the whitetail deer is the number one game animal in the United States. Adaptability and distribution are key factors. But these are the results of conservation programs that took whitetails from a national deer population of 500,000 in 1900 to some 18,000,000 today. Hunter interest in whitetails has never been higher.

Vocal expressions of the whitetails have been observed and studied in great length. Whereas for years grunts and bleats were thought to encompass all deer language, today we know that deer vocalizations fall into four major categories of calls. They are Maternal, Mating, Aggressive, and Distress.

Maternal includes the soft doe grunt, the soft mew nursing whine, and the bleat of a fawn. Mating includes the low-volume grunt made by both bucks and does and the important tending grunt of a trailing or mating buck. Aggressive calls include the grunt-snort, which can be made by buck or doe to challenge rivals, and the back-off-buddy buck call, the grunt-snort-wheeze. Distress calls include the low-pitched snort, which is often accompanied by foot stomping while the whitetail analyzes an uncertain situation, and the high-pitched snort of a fleeing deer. Bawling is the extreme alarm sound of a wounded deer. It is primarily associated with fawns, but mortally wounded adult deer bawl as well. I have witnessed this sound when a newborn fawn was killed by a fox and again as an adult deer was taken down by coyotes.

Whitetail hunters have become more educated and knowledgeable than ever before. Hunters today are more conscious about whitetail ways throughout the autumn. Rubs, scrapes, bedding, feeding, and the travel to-and-from are all important elements when scouting and hunting whitetail-active woods. Today, however, deceiving the whitetail's senses has become focus of the hunt: using camouflage patterns to fool their eyes, applying scent or going scentless to fool their nose and using calls to fool their ears.

Turkey hunters have long practiced a variety of hen and gobbler calls. Elk hunters seriously practice the bull bugling sequence and cow conversation. Whitetail hunters seemed to grasp deer calling, but many of them just bought any old grunt call and tooted at every passing deer without a clue to the language of the animal. But in the last decade, all that changed with increased research and knowledge of the language of the whitetail. What has become evident is the need for a new deer call to provide the educated deer caller a variety of vocalizations.

THE CALLING

David Oathout returned home to the Adirondack Mountains in upstate New York in 1989. David had spent 12 years as a mixed deep sea-saturation diver on demolition and oil rig sites around the world at depths to 1000 feet. The life expectancy of that type of employment is 12 years. David didn't want to press his luck, so he quit while he was even and went home.

"Home," for him, was a small camp near his mother Alma and his stepfather Bob Avery. Avery is a well-known name in the southern Adirondack region as Bob's family homesteaded in the town of Arietta in 1834.

Bob's father Lyman Avery started a guiding business in 1906. Since that time sportsman have associated good hunting with the landmark Avery's Hotel. Into the 1960s large parties of hunters drove big mountains for big deer. In 1962, Bob Avery shot the largest Adirondack black bear, the second largest black bear ever recorded nationally at that time. The 562-lb. (656 lb. estimated live weight) bruiser was the cover story of the May 1963 issue of *Outdoor Life*.

Legendary guide, hunter, and deeryard owner Bob Avery with David Oathout, the inventor of the True Talker. Photo credit: Charles A. Alsheimer.

Bob Avery had always had a fascination with whitetails. In 1967, Avery fenced off a 500-acre mountain across from the hotel and started his own deeryard. David was 13 at the time as brothers, step-brothers, and Avery friends John Olstrem and Larry Hamilton put up three miles of fencing to enclose the yard. To occupy the yard, Avery acquired deer from Pennsylvania and Massachusetts. Upon hearing of the large yarding area, Marlin Perkins of TV's *Wild Kingdom* fame sent deer from Missouri. The deeryard is regionally known for the big bucks that reside there. At one time 140 deer called the mountain home. Today there are 30. It has been a labor of love for the 82-year-old Avery. No matter the weather, the deer still need feeding. Coyotes, black bears and eagles take their share of fawns. But people and poachers have been the problem that closed the yard to the public 5 years ago.

In 1989, when David returned home, he had a new appreciation for the deeryard. Many of the big bucks seen on magazine covers and in the articles within popular hunting magazines are photos taken by top wildlife photographers in the Avery yard. Spending time with the photographers and living among the whitetails on a daily basis made David appreciate the tremendous research facility this deeryard is. It wasn't long before Oathout put the family resource to use and ventured into the deer lure field.

It was while doing lure seminars at outdoor shows in the early 1990s that the idea of a deer call entered his mind. At every seminar people would ask David which deer call they should use. Oathout was well aware that whitetails were capable of more vocalizations than a standard grunt tube could muster. David came to the realization that it was time to tune into the deer tones at home and create a call of his own.

THE TRUE TALKER

As a kid, Oathout hung out with the deer in the yard on a regular basis. He was well aware that deer made vocalizations. David states, "I just grew up knowing deer talked, just as birds sing." He also learned that deer have different personalities, just as people do. Whitetails also possess distinct social habits that hunters must recognize to become successful callers. A calmly feeding September deer is going to act differently from a rut-charged November buck. The calling must match the situation. Fawn mews and the soft, communal grunt are appropriate for calm, early-season deer, whereas deep guttural grunts, the chop of a tending grunt, or a fawn bleat to draw in a doe with a trailing buck is best for the November hunt. Since hunters are much more informed on deer behavior than ever before, David decided that it was time for a call that accurately matched the various deer vocalizations.

Being a hunter, Oathout went right to the source, a dead whitetail deer. By dissecting the trachea and voice

Recognizing the aggressive social behavior of a rutting buck will enable the hunter to employ the appropriate calls like deep guttural grunts, short and choppy tending grunts, or doe bleats, to draw the deer into range.

The True Talker's design allows the user to change calls with the press of a finger.

box, David could see the design of nature's perfect deer call. The challenge was to create a device that could be easily used by man. Many call designs on the market were tube calls with a reed assembly. But the only way to change tone was to manually move the band over the reed by hand, up or down, to change the tone of the call. I used to stop into David's house and find him in his small shop turning out wooden mouthpiece assemblies on his lathe. He worked tirelessly making different wooden voice chambers and reed assemblies until he found the sound he wanted. Corrugated tube the diameter of a deer trachea was used for the call barrel. The texture of the rubber over the barrel also was a consideration for the tone the call would produce. Each step of the way, David would take his work in progress and test it at the deeryard.

Oathout created a call with great tone. But David wanted a versatile call with great tone. And then it came to him: an elliptical cutout running the length of the side of the wooden mouthpiece to expose the reed. When the rubber covering was applied, the tone of the call could be changed with the inflection of the finger. And with adjust-

able memory bands across the flexible reed section, calls tones could be pre-set so a variety of calls could be made without looking at the call. David tirelessly tested his new invention in the deeryard. Oathout says that "it was very exciting when the deer began responding to my calls throughout the duration of the autumn." At last, the True Talker was born.

It was about a decade ago when David invited me up to see his new creation and to present me with a prototype. On an October morning we entered the deeryard and David showed me how to use the call effectively. I immediately knew that this guy had come up with something new and exceptional. A good ol' boy whose determination and ingenuity had come up with a new, refreshing approach to deer calling, Oathout then began selling the calls, as he had sold his lure, at regional outdoor sport shows. The calls sold great.

In 1995, David went to the big show in Harrisburg, Pa, and then onto another large show in Kentucky. While in the Bluegrass State, David was approached by Hunter Specialties, Inc., the country's largest manufacturer of hunting accessories. The rest is history. According to Mike Cannoy at H. S. Calls, more than a half-million True Talker calls have been sold since 1998. That's pretty amazing when you consider that this call started out in a small deer camp in the Adirondacks!

STILL TALKING

During the last decade I have tested a variety of deer calls and always return to the True Talker. It has been a great companion whether using bow, muzzleloader, or rifle. The basic calls I employ the most are the Contented Grunt, a calming call that can also bring in curious deer. For rutting calls I create the choppy "*urp-urp-urp*" for tending bucks, and a deep, guttural grunt for a challenge that I often use with antler rattling. The True Talker is capable of high-pitched fawn bleats and moderate-pitched doe bleats. The call is also capable of a hair-raising deer bawl that I have used to call in a coyote. For more in-depth insight into deer vocalizations and the use of the True Talker, the Outdoor Adventures video *GRUNT-SNORT-WHEEZE* is excellent. The video features phenomenal footage by David Oathout of deer actually making 12 different vocalizations. Dr. Karl Miller, Associate Professor of Wildlife Management at the University of Georgia, narrates the video and explains the calls and the deer's behavior. The video concludes with two-time National Deer Calling Champion Phil Liddle demonstrating the ability and range of the True Talker deer call.

14

Wild Turkeys: The Big Game of Spring

A muzzleloader shotgun and a wild turkey are a perfect match for the traditional hunter, especially when you consider the action that happens on both side of the equation. The muzzleloader hunter creates every shot charge a step at a time, seating the components with the ramrod. The ignition of a muzzleloading firearm, of course, is a show unto itself.

The antics of a spring gobbler, whether it's the visual of a full-blown strutting bird or the audio of pounding gobbles at dawn, are one of nature's marvels. Some of my most cherished spring turkey memories are visions of approaching gobblers, coaxed into range as I peered through the hammers of a percussion shotgun.

A frenzied gobbler is almost a sci-fi character with head turning red-white-blue, wings dragging, puffed-up black-tipped feathers with an iridescent sheen, and a crescent tail fully fanned.

A gobbler's unique drumming is an eerily magical sound. When a rutting tom tees off with a thundering gobble just out of your vision, it's almost unnerving.

CLASSIC IS NOT ALWAYS THE CASE

The classic way to kill a gobbler is to call him from the roost or slip close as he gobbles, then coax him into the effective range of your muzzleloading shotgun. In this day and age, the term "classic" means "rare" or "seldom."

After more than a decade of significant turkey hunting interest and pressure, we have produced an educated game bird. The result: fewer fools rush in. The particular phase of the mating season also affects your spring hunting season. The pre-breeding, hen-gathering phase is a very active time as gobblers compete for hens, making it

The antics of a spring tom turkey are quite a production.

a prime hunting period. Peak breeding season, when the dominant toms are all henned up with their love-stricken harems, can be a quiet time in the turkey woods.

After the hens are bred and nesting, the lone gobblers are again active at the tail end of the breeding season. It's not that you can't still get a gobbler to come running, but

There is a muzzleloading shotgun for every turkey hunter preference. From left to right: Tennessee Valley Muzzleloading 20-ga. Fowler, Dixie Gun Works 10-ga. Magnum Shotgun, the Knight MK-86 12-ga. with a Simmons Whitetail Classic 2x32 scope, and the Thompson/Center 12-ga. Encore.

our new generation of wild turkey will make you earn your trophy. Here are a few common examples of the kind of stunts that today's gobblers typically pull:

• The gobbler you call to on a roost does fly down but moves away from your calls to draw out the hen.

• A tom comes towards your calls but stops, still gobbling, trying to draw out the source of the calls.

• You have a tom gobbling feverishly only to find he is with hens and refuses to leave them for the sounds of an unseen lonely hen in the bush.

• Silent, call-shy toms try to sneak up on hen calls to see if the source is really an unattended hen.

TACTICS AND STRATEGY

The essence of spring turkey hunting is the exchange of calls between the hunter and a located gobbler. Locating a gobbler is the first step in spring hunting. Roosting the turkeys at night is the surest way to have a tom located for morning. Wing beats and cackling at dusk are dead giveaways to a roosting site.

To pinpoint a gobbler at dusk or dawn, a locator call is used. Crow, hawk, gobbler and owl calls are traditional roosting-bird locators and are used to persuade a tom to gobble from his roost. Educated birds in heavily hunted areas may not respond to commonly used locator calls. Many hunters now carry a shrill peacock call, or a silent dog whistle for just that reason.

If you are able to locate a tom at dusk, you will know exactly where you want to be in the pre-dawn darkness in the morning. If not, you will start out your morning in search of a roosted tom, using your locator call until full daylight when the birds begin leave their roosts. Then it's time to hen call to the roaming breeding gobblers and "wannabe" (henless) gobblers of spring. You will find that the wannabe breeders provide the best action whether they come in gobbling or just sneak in for a peak at a potentially unattended hen.

Locating a tom is only the first move in the chess game. Then the calling exchange begins. Every bird will be different. Some will run right in. Some will fuss a long time before coming in. And some will never come in. As a turkey hunter you must be proficient with a variety of calling devices and be able to create a variety of turkey language. From wing bone calls to box calls, to peg and slate, to shaker gobbler calls, to the mouth diaphragm, the turkey hunter should be comfortable with, and capable of making, the basic turkey sounds. The only way you will learn is to practice and play with a selection of calls. You should be able to yelp, the most widely used language of turkeys. Soft clucks and putts express contentment where loud putts signal alarm. A purr following yelps is often the clincher on a close tom. On the rare occasion when challenging a gobbler or shocking a tom into calling, use a gobbler call. And don't be afraid to improvise with natural

From yelping with a mouth diaphragm call to scratching the leaves on the ground to sound like a feeding hen, the hunter needs to be creative with calls and natural sounds to fool a tom.

sounds such as scratching at the leaves to replicate the sound of a hen uncovering new spring shoots. Listening to preseason turkeys is the best way to hear their vocabulary and to understand what each "word" means and when it is used.

IMPROVE AS A HUNTER

I have seriously hunted wild turkeys for the last dozen years, and I've had some marvelous encounters while muzzleloading for spring turkeys. But it has only been the last five years that I have become a better turkey hunter. How? Through observations of turkey behavior while photographing them. I discovered just how little I knew about the social structure and daily routine of the wild turkeys of spring. Roost gobbling and subsequent fly-down are only a fraction of the activities of this animated game bird. It didn't take me long to realize that the wild turkey could and should be hunted just as we hunt their fall counterpart, the whitetail deer. Scouting for feeding areas, bedding areas, rutting zones, and the trails connecting them are second nature to the whitetail hunter geared for success. So why wasn't I taking the time to scout for spring gobblers the same way?

Photographing the wild turkey is pre-season hunting with a camera. I found roosting areas, set up my photo blind and planned pictures. Over the course of these clandestine photo shoots, I became familiar with the daily routine of a wild turkey. Fly-down occurs only after there is enough light to let the turkey discern a safe landing area. No matter how big or small the band of birds is, flock organization occurs after all the turkeys are on the ground. Toms then gather and begin strutting. The "flock" hen organizes the rest of the birds through loud vocal assertiveness and confrontation if needed. Fly-down period and flock organization can be one loud ruckus at first light.

Once organized, the flock heads to the first feeding location of the day. This is when toms and hens begin to break off into smaller groups. Strutting and courting occur during this early period. Bands of jakes circle the area and stay clear of the big toms. The first three hours of daylight see the largest period of mating activity as the flock moves along like a miniature herd of caribou.

By mid-morning, most breeding activities have already occurred. Hens disperse to nest and toms begin roaming for unattended, interested hens. The daily routine at mid-day finds single hens near their nests, hens banded together, jakes banded together, and small groups and single mature gobblers scattered about. When the hens wander away, the gobblers follow them. This wandering period of mid-morning through mid-afternoon takes the splinter groups of interested suitors through other feeding areas and dusting areas for their daily baths. Dusting areas, like early morning fly-down zones, are excellent strutting zones. The daily activities conclude with the birds feeding their way back to their roosting area at dusk.

FINDING THE RIGHT PLACE

Scouting should be conducted a couple of weeks prior to the spring turkey season and continue right up to opening day and all the days that you hunt. This way you can keep tabs on the changing activities of the breeding season. There will be a transition from pre-breeding mixed flocks, to the harem-gathering period where toms are at peak gobbling and strutting, to breeding flocks where gobblers have no pressing need to announce their presence, to deserted gobblers who again actively gobble and patrol because all the harem hens are nesting. No matter which phase of the mating season you find the turkeys in when opening day arrives, their core area will remain the same. By finding their areas for roosting, feeding, strutting, and dusting, you can pattern their movements and intercept them along the way.

Wild turkey scouting consists of locating tracks, scratchings made by feeding, and droppings. You'll also want to keep your eyes open for strutting zones and dusting bowls. Tracks of mature gobblers are noticeably larger than hen tracks and have middle toes measuring 2-1/2 to 3-1/2 inches long. Fresh turkey droppings are moist and green with a dash of white. Gobbler droppings are in the shape of a J while hen droppings are round and spiraled.

Scratchings are where turkeys rake the ground for old mast including acorns, green shoots, and insects. Dusting bowls are shallow, oval depressions in dry dirt areas. Since bathing and preening occur in dusting areas, look for feathers strewn about, especially the black-tipped breast feathers of gobblers. Strutting marks are shallow, narrow grooves made by the tips of a gobbler's primary feathers as he puffs up and parades, dragging his wings.

By the start of spring turkey season, you should already have noted when and where you saw turkeys and turkey sign at common roosting, feeding, dusting, and strutting areas.

This tom and hens just hit the ground after flying off their roost. The hens will head to the first feeding area of the day where the gobbler will strut and court hens.

Even though you are shooting a shotgun, a tom turkey's head is a very small target. This 12–ga. T/C Black Mountain Magnum Turkey Shotgun topped with a T/C 1.25-4 x 32 scope was loaded with 100 gr. of Pyrodex Select, two Wonder Wads over powder, and two oz. of #6 copper-plated shot topped with an over-shot wad.

By intercepting the turkey's spring travels the author was able to coax this bird within muzzleloader shotgun range. (Note the two-compartment speed loaders that contain powder and shot, the felt wads, and 209 shotgun primers that fed and fired this camo-clad, break-action T/C Encore.)

HUNTING THE RIGHT TIME

My turkey hunting has primarily consisted of calling roosted birds, and then walking and calling until a talking tom answers. It took an older experienced turkey hunter to teach me to hunt turkey travel routes the same way you would hunt whitetail trails. He scouted and glassed strutting gobblers and their open field locations prior to the season. One Saturday he took a gobbler with a 10-½-inch beard, and the following Saturday a gobbler with a 12-inch beard. The hunter scored by putting decoys in view of a strutting zone and hiding in the corner of the field. Every 15 to 30 minutes he did some light hen calling. Between mid-morning and noon each day the lonely gobblers strutted right into shooting range.

This past spring I set my father up in a ground blind in a daily feeding area between a roosting area and a dusting/strutting zone. With decoys set at 20 yards my father lightly hen-called at intervals. Several hens passed my father's blind and a gobbler taunted him by calling several times just up the ridge. My father adjusted his stand location and decoys to the gobbler's travel route for the following morning's hunt. At 11:30 a.m., my father was looking through the hammers of his 10-gauge shotgun at the largest turkey he had ever seen: a 22-pound gobbler sporting a 10-inch beard.

CONCLUSION

Getting the drop on the toms of spring means doing your preseason homework. It is the observation and knowledge of your intended gobbler's daily routine that will put you in the right place at the right time. It requires less use of the call but more strategic thinking in terms of stand locations and more use of the eyes and ears. It consists of setting up decoys so the gobbler has to pass your concealed location, and then letting the gobbler come to you.

On the last day of spring turkey season I put this tactic to the test. The sun was above the horizon by the time I got set up in a woodland opening between a hardwood ridge and a swamp. A light, moving fog turned my decoy as the dew burned off. A half hour later a gobbler approached from the timber above. At 75 yards he began to gobble at the two hen decoys. Suddenly a thundering gobble came from the swamp edge. Like book ends, the two full-blown gobblers approached the hens and each other. The uphill bird was walking right into the path of my shotgun. When the smoke lifted my first thought was, what a show!

15

Tree Hoppers And High Fliers

BARKING FOR BUSHYTAILS

Gray squirrel seasons are generally long and liberal. It is a proven fact that hunters have little impact on the prolific gray squirrel. But like all game animals, you need to know their habits and traits to be successful–especially when attempting to hunt them with muzzleloading firearms. Achieving effective range is the hunter's toughest task. Glimpses of an agile gray blur leaping from one swaying branch to another is not the shot you're looking for. Knowledge of your shooting iron and its capabilities will determine your safety and success afield. Hunting with a .22 rifle at this time of year has always been an extremely effective method to take a good number of squirrels and hone one's shooting skills. For new, young hunters and their dads, squirrel hunting provides the action needed for fun, quality outings.

The 32-cal. Traditions Crockett Small Game Rifle is a 49-inch percussion half-stock with a 32-inch barrel, fixed blade sights, and double set triggers for the soft touch this small game target requires. Traditional, clean lines make this a very stylish small-caliber muzzleloader that looks right at home in the squirrel woods. The Crockett has enough drop in its walnut stock to shoulder comfortably and the sights align easily. The barrel is long enough for steady offhand shooting. This lean small-bore is easy to cradle across the arm and fun to shoot as it cracks in the hardwoods.

Blackpowder in the FFFg granulation or Pyrodex P grade are the only acceptable propellants to be used in the Crockett rifle. The load my father and I settled upon consists of CCI #11 magnum percussion caps, 20 grains of Goex FFFg blackpowder, 32-cal. cotton shooting patches from Traditions lubricated with liquid dish soap and a .310 Hornady swaged round ball. The 1:48 twist in the

Gray squirrel action can enhance the skill of the new hunter and the seasoned marksman.

32-inch blued barrel gave good results off a bench rest as we sighted in dead-on at a realistic offhand/open sights shooting range of 25 yards. At 50 yards the shots hit a little over an inch low.

The 32-cal. Traditions Crockett Small Game Rifle is right at home in the squirrel woods.

Only range time that includes measuring powder charges, patch lubing, ball starting and loading, and off-hand practice with your muzzleloading firearm will demonstrate how to load efficiently and shoot accurately. Bore preparation is a must when shooting through the constricted space of a small-bore barrel. Fouled barrels in small calibers contribute to difficult loading. A clean, clear, flash channel and barrel are the first steps toward successful shooting and safe hunting. Traditions' 32-cal.

Durable Range Rod accepts cleaning accessories including a jag and a brush.

Squirrel habitat usually consists of semi-open terrain. Softwoods with adjacent mast foods or planted crops are the norm. And if you can add a small creek to that setting, you are in prime bushytail cover. The first thing you should do is to examine the area for squirrels or signs of squirrels. Autumn will find grays on the ground gathering nuts to bury for winter. When you find freshly-gnawed nut hulls, chewed corn at a field edge, or winter holes in the snow from food searches, you have found the squirrels.

Blending in with your surroundings and seeing the grays before they see you is the name of the game. I wear camouflage and my drop-seat turkey vest. This way I can sit and be comfortable on a moment's notice. Looking and listening is your first tactic. Listen for squirrel calls such as barking, rustling of leaves of moving game, and the nut gnawing of a feeding squirrel. Look for obvious squirrels moving on the ground and in the trees. Then use your compact binoculars to search for bushytails sitting tight to trunks, or laying out flat on branches.

In the last few years I have taken to calling squirrels by imitating the barking calls. The basic squirrel bark is produced with a bellows type call. It consists of a rubber bellows connected to a tube. The tube is held in one hand while the other rhythmically taps the bellows to create squirrel barks, the common communicating call. This is excellent for sneaking into an area and calling. The call is also good for use after scaring a gray away. Just sit tight for fifteen minutes and lightly call. The inquisitive gray will soon reappear. Rhythmic barking is my favorite way to call. Another use for the bellows is when you first enter an area. Shake the bellows to create the alarm chatter. This can create some fast action as squirrels run to trees, climb up, and always stop to look for the danger. Squirrel Call effectively produces the bark of a squirrel as a large wooden opening on the bellows permits greater control and varied tones.

A real attention getter is the high-pitched distress squeal. And, just as in calling predators, the more distressed-sounding you are, the better. To produce the squeal, form a fist and suck at the hole formed by the forefinger and the thumb. You will learn to vary the pitch by opening and closing the other three fingers of your hand. Thrashing bushes or branches while squealing will complete the scenario of a squirrel in the clutches of a predator. This can really stir up the local bushytail population as the inquisitive tree dwellers get out on the branches for a look.

GUNNING FOR GEESE

While some waterfowl fly purposefully to wintering grounds, large, lordly Canadas travel the flyways in a leisurely fashion. If they can find a preferred food source and a desirable safe-haven body of water, they will stay and work an area's food source until it is depleted or a weather front preceding a cold snap moves them along. Dairy farming and cornfields are synonymous along the Mohawk Valley. Unfortunately the farms aren't as numerous as they once were, but there are still large expanses of the deep shade of yellow ripe corn called maize. It is not so much the corn itself as it is the mechanical marvel that picks the corn each autumn that makes corn stubble and the attendant debris the Canada's favorite choice for nutritious dining. The once tasseled, towering corn stalks are chopped and obliterated, leaving kernels, cobs, and stalk pulp strewn about vast acreages of open stubble fields.

Knight & Hale's squirrel calls and instructional video will help you get started barking for bushytails.

The DGW 10-ga. magnum with chrome-lined barrels for non-toxic shot was the first muzzleloader Gary Stoller had ever fired at a goose.

Magnum goose shells are excellent for hunters to hide under as geese begin their approach to a decoy spread.

Shooting geese over decoys is exciting and fun. The spectacle of a flock of geese setting their wings and pitching down into a field is a visual event that has to be experienced at close range to be appreciated. If you've got a gun in your hands when this happens, it's even better! Canada geese do make an impressive sight as they turn into the wind and curve their wings, pitching down to settle among the decoys.

Of all the goose hunting Gary Stoller has done, he had never fired at one with a muzzleloader. So we loaded up the Dixie Gun Works 10-ga. magnum with 100 gr. of Goex FFg blackpowder pushing 1-½ ounces of #6 Hevi-Shot. The non-toxic shot patterned well in the chrome-lined barrels out to 30-yards using one Ox-Yoke Wonder Wad over powder and one over shot. The DGW 10 gauge is a handsome half-stock shotgun featuring wrist checkering and cheek-piece on the satin finished European walnut stock with a comfortable two-inch drop at the heel. The 30-inch chrome-lined browned barrels feature cylinder bore (right) and a modified (left) fixed chokes. The beautifully engraved locks appropriately feature flying Canada geese. This 7-½-pound, 46-½-inch shotgun is a truly handsome muzzleloading shotgun. From all varieties of upland birds to hefty wild turkeys, my father and I have taken a significant amount of game with this shotgun.

The sky was clear on the November morning that Gary and I headed across the muddy corn stubble field with decoys in tow on a plastic sled. Gary had observed several flocks on consecutive days grazing in this field. The amount of goose droppings between the rows of stubble let us know they had been here. The amount of corn kernels and cobs still strewn about let us know the geese would be back.

We had the decoys set and our ground cloths spread when Gary heard the first lone flyer of the morning. The goose made a circle of the field and moved on. Then the first flock appeared in the distance. With his Knight & Hale call, Gary began calling loudly, repeating the familiar *huuuuurooonk* again and again. Flocks suddenly materialized coming from both the big lake to the north and the river to the south. At all different elevations there were large flocks and small bands of geese in the air above our decoy spread. The sound of the Canadas' honking was unbelievably loud. Several clusters of geese began their slow slide down to investigate the decoys. Suddenly, wing beats right overhead surprised us. The large waterfowl looked almost as they were lumbering along. But as soon as Gary popped out from under his magnum goose shell those birds were past us before we could react. We were trying to sit tight until a 30-yard shot materialized. There were so many geese in the sky, flying high, passing low, and circling, that we never saw these birds until it was too late.

During the next hour several more flocks came in low, but not low enough for a shot with the DGW big

10. Watching the height of ground behind me, Gary had noticed that geese from the north were passing quite close to the ground at that particular spot. At that moment the sky was clear. It was obvious the morning's action was winding down. The decision was made to leave the decoys right where they were and the two of us take cover in the fence line where the low flyers were surprising us.

We had barely got in position when geese were upon us. Gary stood up, pointed the shotgun at the nearest goose and fired. The "easy" looking goose hovering overhead flew off unscathed. The very next flock that turned to approach the decoys sailed right over our heads, treetop high. This time the shooter was swinging on a goose. And this time when the front bead passed the bird's beak, the shooter touched off the left, modified barrel of the 10-ga. The 10-lb. Canada goose dropped like a rock, and Gary at last became a confirmed blackpowder goose hunter.

Leaving the decoys in place and moving to the fence line produced the goose of the morning.

16

Favorite Guns For A Favorite Pastime

It is safe to say that I was brought up bird hunting. For 43 of my 49 years my father and a bird dog have provided me with decades of outdoor fun and adventure. Over the years Brittany spaniels, English setters and English springer spaniels have put into flight a fair amount of quail, woodcock, partridge, pheasants and chuckars for our shotguns. Having been exposed to bird dogs most of my life, I have discovered one thing: whether they pointed or flushed, each breed and each dog possessed unique traits. Some dogs were born bird hunters, some were molded into bird hunters, and some were bird dogs by name only. I also learned that it is a lot more fun hunting birds that it is hunting bird dogs. But the rewards are many when you find a natural bird dog that was born to please. There is rarely, if ever, a bad day afield if you have a dog who likes to hunt with you.

A NEW BEGINNING

"We don't need a check–we're just going to look," I told my wife Chris on a February day in 1994. It had been a year since the passing of our last dog, and my parent's setter was getting on in years. Chris and I had discovered the breeder of the Springer spaniel that I hunted with from the time I was 12 to age 24. I truly adored that dog. You were never alone when you hunted with ol' Sam.

We arrived at the breeder's residence and were shown their show champion line of springers that are much more marketable as show dogs than hunting dogs. Several black and white cuties ran in circles and played. Over in the corner was a liver and white pup in a separate cage. We asked about the pup. The breeder opened the cage door. Without hesitation the little springer crossed the room, passed her playing bundle of brethren, and softly hopped up in my lap. With her front paws on my chest she looked

The author's father smiles proudly after a successful hunt with his setter Kate.

Sadie was raised flushing birds for a pair of Dixie doubles.

right into my eyes like no other dog I have known.

We named her Sadie.

RAISED ON BLACKPOWDER

Dad and I had begun using muzzleloading shotguns for our fall bird hunting in the late 1980s, and we were well entrenched in the habit by the time Sadie arrived in '94. My father greeted her with some partridge feathers that Sadie sniffed so hard they stuck to her nose.

Sadie was a pleasure to train from the get-go. She had mastered the main commands–sit, stay, heel, and come–by spring. Field-work on a check cord was pleasing as the springer naturally quartered side to side 30 to 50 feet out. She was easy, and gentle, and attentive. Soon the command "come-round" had her running to me.

My father began taking her to the skeet range to watch and listen to the shooters. She didn't even pay any notice. Then she cruised through the finding and flushing of birds set in spring traps, with a cap gun shooting during flush. By September it was time to shoot some birds over her at a local pheasant preserve. My father said, "Why don't we just start her out with a blackpowder shotgun?" It wasn't long before the new pup associated the flush of a bird and the sound of a muzzleloading shotgun with something exciting. The rest is history.

Twenty-, 12-, and 10-ga. shotguns, single barrel and double, flintlock and percussion, have dropped birds over Sadie's flushes. It's so easy to tell when she gets birdy. Her body language always gives it away. The liver and white dog with the orange Quick-Spot vest methodically works covers. When Sadie's pace quickens she's onto scent; when she's leaning into it she's trailing; and when her ears perk up and her head alertly pops up, she has a visual. And being true to her spaniel genes, with a pounce Sadie springs the bird into flight. Muzzles blast, smoke belches skyward, and Sadie lunges forward in hopes of hearing "Downed bird, hunt 'em up!" This friend and field companion born in the fall of '93 is now the veteran of 10 great hunting seasons.

A TOUGH SEASON FOR A SEASONED DOG

Bird season found the hunting conditions warm, dry and windy in the northeast. For a bird dog this is tough sledding: tough scenting game, tough trailing game, and tough finding downed game. But it was bird season and we were hunting. A high, bowl-shaped farm field seemed to have the elements that pheasants desired: food, cover and water. The farmer who lets us run Sadie on his land informed us that he had heard pheasants cackling at daybreak on several occasions. Since there was very little

activity in our normal partridge and woodcock haunts we jumped at the chance. And when it comes to wild, open terrain pheasants, my father and I carry our favorite pair, Dixie Gun Works double barrel shotguns in 10 and 20-ga.

Sadie was just thrilled to actually get onto some fresh, abundant bird scent. Down in an alder bottom she worked a pheasant that ran and ran. I got glimpses of it in a fencerow. Suddenly a dark brown, crouching object moved left to right up a bank in the waist-high grasses. At the fencerow, the deer stood up and jumped over it, almost landing in my father's pocket. Naturally, at that moment the wild pheasant safely took to flight. That was just the beginning of four pheasant hunts that produced just two birds that my father took with the DGW big 10 double. But what frustrated both the bird dog and muzzleloader hunters most was the persistent wind that ranged from 10 to 30 mph on a given day.

On one such day Sadie trailed a hen pheasant for several hundred yards through dense undergrowth. At the corner of two hedgerows Sadie's ears perked and she leaped over a log and under a grape vine tangle. A raucous cackling from the other side sounded, and I lifted my eyes in time to see a handsome, cagey cock pheasant fly over the cattails distant. The downwind bird was moving much faster than normal as I swung on the flying target. But I rolled the pheasant with the left Improved cylinder barrel of the DGW 20-ga. double. The bird disappeared 30 yards away over the hedgerow. We searched the area methodically for a half hour. The air-washed bird had left no scent for Sadie to find. It was the first bird in her career we were unable to recover. It was just another difficult day in an unusually difficult season.

Whether sitting tight, running hedgerows, or cackling into flight, pheasants are great game birds for the muzzleloading shotgunner.

BASIC SHOOTING FUNDAMENTALS EQUAL SUCCESS

When things aren't going well it is not uncommon to question your tactics and ability. Birds flying with and against a stiff wind can test the skill of any shooter. The distance and the angle of the shot only add to the degree of difficulty. It is very common to undercompensate for birds flying with the wind and overcompensate for those flying against it. It's like shooting a round of skeet and then shooting a round of trap. It is all a matter of timing, making the adjustment as you come up behind the target, accelerate through, and shoot at the appropriate lead. The key to success for the "swing through" shooter is in understanding the delays in the shooting process on unpredictable targets.

Hitting a flying target with a muzzleloading shotgun is a three-step procedure. Step one is reacting to the appearance of the target and shouldering your gun. Step two is the mechanical process of squeezing the trigger, which is followed by an unavoidable delay as the hammer falls and the powder charge is ignited. Step three is following the target with the barrel(s) and ultimately swinging through it so that the shot charge intersects it before the pattern becomes too diffuse. Firing at the right time and a strong follow-through are essential for successful muzzleloader wingshooting.

Mike Jardine with a Dixie double pheasant.

HOW TO LOAD A DIXIE DOUBLE

It was the Tuesday after Thanksgiving when we met up with friend Mike Jardine for a pheasant hunt. Mike has succeeded on several muzzleloading whitetails with his traditional .50 T/C Hawken rifle. He now wanted to give a muzzleloading shotgun a try on pheasants. At this point, my father and I just wanted a decent day to hunt. A few birds to reward Sadie's efforts would be nice as well.

My father proceeded to show Mike the loading process for the Dixie doubles. As a clean, dry barrel and ignition port is essential for all successful muzzleloader shooting, my father wiped the barrels with Ox-Yoke Original's shotgun cleaning rod and patches. Then, with the cleaning rod and patch seated in the barrel a #11 percussion cap was snapped to clear nipples and flash channels. When the cleaning rod was removed, the cap-fouled patch indicated a clear flash channel.

The pheasant load chain we use for the DGW 10-ga.double is 90 gr. of Goex FFg blackpowder, two Ox-Yoke Originals Wonder Wads, and 1-¼ oz. of #5 shot topped with another Wonder Wad. The DGW 20-ga. double load chain consists of 70 gr. of FFg, two Wonder Wads, and 1 oz. of #6 shot topped with a Wonder Wad. Both loads are the traditional volume-for-volume shotgun load. The shot charge is the volume equivalent of the powder charge. We tried and tested these loads and have used them with confidence for 10 years.

My father also showed Mike how to keep the ramrod in one of the barrels while loading a double. This way there's little risk of accidentally double-charging a barrel, which can be disastrous. We carry our powder and shot in pre-measured speed loads, our wads in a separate container, and the #11s in a capper on a lanyard around our necks. For safety, the capped guns are carried in the half-cock position.

A DIXIE DOUBLE DAY

Thunder Meadows Shooting Preserve in Westerlo, N. Y., is a Morgan horse retirement farm where the crops are farmed and groomed for pheasants and pheasant hunting, making it a great playground for bird dogs and muzzleloading shotgun enthusiasts. In this day and age of habitat loss to urban sprawl, particularly in the northeast, quality shooting preserves are the last bastion of fun and games on game-rich grounds for bird dogs and their masters. Even our woodcock and grouse covers in the southern Adirondack region are aged and depleted. Top that off with the influx of eastern coyotes with red wolf in their gene pool, and you have an efficient, intelligent predator that just loves snacking on ground nesting birds. Let's just say that the good old days of bird hunting in the Adirondacks aren't "now," they're "then."

There was something very good and different about this late November bird hunt. The ground was damp from recent rains, the sky was partly cloudy, the temperature

Sadie with the rewards of her favorite pastime.

was a perfect-for-hunting 45 degrees, and there was just a gentle stir of air. Even before we had the guns ready, Sadie was walking with head held high as she winded game along the fencerow by the truck. I manned the camera as my father and Mike headed for the first covers of fox grass and sorghum. We circled to get Sadie downwind of the cover. The hunters walked the edges as Sadie quartered before them. Suddenly, the bird dog was all business as she moved ahead briskly, pausing, and pouncing. Brilliant red wattles against a deep green head atop a white ring led a flaming orange body and pluming tail feathers above the tall, waving grasses. My father swung upon the flushed, rising pheasant and let rip the DGW big 10's right cylinder-choke barrel. Sadie burst forward to claim the downed bird as a large smoke ring lifted.

I vested the pheasant as we moved on in hopes of Mike getting an opportunity. It wasn't long. As another stretch of cover near standing corn came to an end Sadie began working in feverish circles. With no place to hide and Sadie bearing down, another pheasant flushed low and away, presenting a crossing shot to Mike. The new gunner swung the slim DGW 20 through the flying target and dropped the pheasant like an old pro. My father and I quickly commented that this was our season high combined. We began rotating guns and the morning only got better.

Sadie trailed, Sadie chased, and Sadie flushed. One cock bird thought he could outrun the liver and white springer over a stone wall. Sadie cleared the wall on the run and landed on a barbed wire fence that flipped her into a backwards summersault. She hit the ground running and flushed the bird, which I dropped with the DGW 20. I even got another pheasant off a Sadie flush with the DGW 10. It was a perfect morning that ended with my father dropping our fifth and final pheasant. Sadie was one happy hunting dog, in a canine state of euphoric exhaustion. The Dixie doubles were sooted many times over. And the muzzleloader hunters, new and old, finally felt a sense of achievement after a long season of uneventful hunts. At last: an exciting day of traditional pheasant hunting with our favorite springer spaniel flushing for our favorite Dixie doubles.

17

A Test Of Tracking And Shooting Skill: Cottontails And Snowshoes

THE COTTONTAIL

For mid- to late-winter outings when the bird and buck seasons of autumn have passed, the cottontail provides a challenge for the muzzleloading hunter. Whether you track and jump-shoot these hyperactive rabbits with a shotgun or track and shoot sitting rabbits with a rifle, hunting bunnies with a muzzleloader is good sport. Like countless young hunters, my hunting career started with rabbits over beagles. There have been a lot of happy days in the field in this country spent with fathers, sons, baying beagles and bunnies. But as I got older and discovered muzzleloading, the tracking of rabbits in snow and putting yourself in position for a shot with the primitive firearm became my favorite way to bag bunnies.

What makes the cottontail rabbit a worthy object is its ability to survive, which depends upon its knowledge of every path, rock, bush and burrow in its area. A couple of acres are enough for a female cottontail while a male has a larger range. Although cottontails will use the burrows of others for safety, they much prefer to blend in by sitting inside a form. This is a spot that is usually well hidden in a bent clump of grass or briars in a thicket, a fallen treetop or a brush pile. This gives the rabbit a choice, when danger approaches, of either sitting tight or bursting from cover at high speed and rocketing down one of their trails.

The cottontail's sense of hearing is excellent. Their eyes are those of prey, being large and protruding from the side of their head, providing near-comprehensive lateral vision. It is thought that their sense of smell is used primarily for locating food. Rabbits are not openly vocal except for their air-piercing squall of distress.

The cottontail is a small animal, having an overall length of about 14 to 19 inches, and standing 6 to 7 inches high at the shoulder. Weight can vary from 2 to 3 lbs.,

There have been a lot of happy hunting days in the field spent with fathers, sons, baying beagles, and bunnies.

with females being slightly larger than males. Cottontails are brown with a buff or reddish cast, with black-tipped guard hairs. Their belly, chin, inner legs, and, of course, their round little tails are cottony white. Cottontail rabbits are distributed in several varieties across North America. Their noted rapid reproduction rarely puts them in short supply. Whether the rabbits are hunted or not, only 15 to 20 percent survive until the following spring.

The best place to look for cottontails is in the environment where they thrive best: in scrub or brushy landscape of edge covers. The cottontail leaves its best sign after a fresh night's snowfall. Brown droppings stand out against the snow. Gnawing and stripping of the bark of shrubs and trees along the rabbit's trail are good indicators, as are fresh tracks.

Jump-shooting cottontails with a blackpowder shotgun is fast-action fun.

The cottontail will quickly snap you to your senses when one bursts from its cover with front feet landing first, then its hind feet landing ahead of the front, compressing the rabbit's body for its next bound. At top speed, a cottontail can cover as much as 15 feet at a jump. Occasionally, they make a high observation leap in dense cover to check their surroundings. The best thing about a jumped cottontail is that it isn't going to go far, and its tracks are fresh.

I started my muzzleloader hunting the same way my father introduced me to the sport of hunting in general: on cottontail rabbits. I loved to track animals and was really becoming interested in primitive arms hunting. My introduction to muzzleloader hunting success came while still-hunting cottontails. Finally tracking up and making the difficult shot brought a real sense of accomplishment. On the way to that first success more than 25 years ago, I made my share of mistakes. My cottontail still-hunting led me along many a fresh track with a half-stock T/C Seneca .45. The gun was loaded with a 175-gr. patched round ball pushed by 65 gr. of FFg blackpowder. I tracked rabbits on foot and on snowshoes. Learning to sort out the tracks made by the one rabbit I was hunting from the billion surrounding tracks was tough. But spotting a rabbit in its hunkered-down posture before it spotted me was even tougher. A white tail bounding through a berry

patch was often the result. But tracking and successfully still-hunting cottontails, by making exact head or shoulder shots, turned out to be one of muzzleloading's simple lessons, one that would lead to bigger and better things in the deer woods.

SHOTGUN FUN

My favorite approach to cottontails is jump-shooting with a muzzleloading shotgun. Jump-shooting requires fast and accurate handling of a scattergun at a fast-moving, bounding target. Not only is this great action, but it also keeps the upland bird hunter in the swing of things as he follows the dodging target across the varying landscape. This is the most widespread manner of taking cottontails, whether it is with modern or muzzleloading scattergun. Jump-shooting rabbits with the muzzleloading scattergun lets you cruise the rabbit trails instead of tracking at a slow pace. It also gives the hunter the option of shooting at a still target if offered or getting on and swinging through a cottontail that suddenly takes to flight. And take to flight he will. Unlike the still-hunter who unintentionally pushes the rabbit into action, the jump-shooter jumps or scares the cottontail into action. Whether out from under the boughs of a tree or the edges of a brush pile, cottontails waste no time when taking their leave. This often provides fast-paced shooting at a surprised and frequently erratic target. It is for this reason that for jump-shooting I prefer the double-barreled shotgun.

There are some nice single-barreled muzzleloading shotguns on the market today, but for close-quarters bunny jumping, I prefer a double barrel. It only took one rabbit to completely circle me to form my opinion. The Dixie Gun Works 20-ga. double has been a frequent field companion. For a rabbit load, the gun has shot well with an old-time volume-for-volume load of 70 gr. FFg Goex blackpowder pushing the shot volume equivalent of 1oz. of #6 shot. Ox-Yoke Original Wonder Wads are used over the powder with Circle-Fly overshot cards holding everything together. This load was patterned at 30 yards. Smaller shot can be used, too, but I prefer #6 because of its greater mass, deeper penetration, and tighter pattern at close range.

Cottontail rabbits are a plentiful and available small game animal. For those who love to track and hunt, post-deer season cottontails will give you many days of good tracking conditions in brushy areas and woodland edges. But for those seeking a bigger challenge, the snowshoe hare fits the bill.

THE SNOWSHOE HARE

The snowshoe hare broke out ahead of me as I attempted to navigate through a dogwood tangle that had a firm grip on me. The running track of the rabbit soon began to overlap itself as it leaped across a small creek and we began our second big circle. The fresh dusting of

Tracking is an acquired skill that needs to be practiced to be mastered.

February snow made the job easier to decipher which set of tracks were this lap's. We were pivoting around a hemlock swamp and the lanky, white rabbit was staying just far enough ahead that I could get glimpses of him, but not long enough to take aim and shoot. The large-footed rabbit with built-in snowshoes was comfortable with its pace while I shushed along in my snowshoes in the many layers of late winter snow. Onward I plowed, well aware of the tracking and shooting skills the snowshoe rabbit requires.

Approaching a small rise that extended towards the end of the swamp where we were headed, I paused. Since our last lap had brought us around and up the other side of this rise, I thought I might ease up and take a peek over the height of ground. Growing along the top of the quarter-mile-long, narrow stretch of land were clumps of hemlock whose boughs hung low from the accumulation of a long winter's snow. Using these as cover, I was never suspected by the white rabbit as I picked out its dark eye against the sea of snow.

The varying hare's radar ears went into action as I drew back the hammer on my rifle. I flexed my forefinger and the small caliber muzzleloader cracked. A white blur made a hasty departure along the well-traveled rabbit troth. A crease in the snow was the evidence of my missed shot beneath the rabbit. Even though I was disappointed with my missed opportunity, I was glad that I was working the kinks out of my shooting and tracking skills now. Making this kind of mistake next whitetail season would be much more disappointing.

The varying hare, true to its name, is camouflaged for all seasons as it changes from a summer coat of brown to a winter coat of white. The snowshoe rabbit, as they are referred to in my neck of the woods, provides a great winter alternative for the blackpowder hunter. Like the whitetail, the snowshoe rabbit relies on its acute hearing, sight and smell to warn it of danger. The white rabbit's habitat and territorial range are a scaled-down version of the whitetail's. Both the hare and the deer eat the same types of food. Alder thickets and conifer-clad swamps, with their dense undergrowth, provide both food and protection from the elements and predators. Typical habitat is moist woodlands, with hemlock and balsam fir growing over rocks and boulders. Within the boundaries of this habitat, these large rabbits seldom travel more than 1000 feet in any direction as they use every physical feature to their advantage whether feeding or hiding. Low bush hemlock, ground ferns, lichens growing on trunk bark, and the mosses growing on stumps and logs are winter dining favorites. A snowshoe rabbit trail will lead you along their dining buffet that can also include the whips of poplar, ash, and maple as well as their favorite, white cedar. Competition with wintering deer for available foods can limit the hare population.

In the Adirondack foothills, productive white rabbit hunting can be found close to home. The attrition rate of these rabbits is amazing as up to 70% of the adult hares can die annually. White rabbits are very cyclical and known for their population boom and bust periods. Besides the fact that they are challenging and fun to hunt on snowshoes, these white ghosts of winter aren't bad eating either. Pinpoint shot placement is what the snowshoe rabbit demands of the rifle hunter. A sitting rabbit appears to have no neck. The average white rabbit is around 20 inches in length, is 8 to 9 inches tall at the shoulder, and weighs on the average, 2 to 4 lbs. The track of the varying hare stands out from all other tracks because of the wide snowshoe form of the hind foot. The 5 ½-inch long snowshoe on this rabbit looks out of proportion but serves its purpose well by carrying the winter hare over snow its predators can't travel, at speeds up to 30 miles per hour or about 44 feet per second.

Snowshoe rabbit habitat has a trail system just as whitetail deer have their common trails through preferred feeding and bedding areas. Hare trails in winter can become ruts in the mounting snow that can hide all but its eyes and ears. If you happen into the same cover in the absence of snow, you will find the same trail ruts in the ground. Whitetail tracks reveal a creature of habit travelling between food, water and bedding. These worn trails indicate repeated activities. So do the network of trails of the snowshoe rabbit. The varying hare feeds mainly at night, but he is also very active on dark, overcast days. These are the best days to track and hunt as the diffused light of the overcast sky gives much better definition of the shadow and shape of tracks, as well as the white rabbit's outline against the snow.

HUNTING ON SNOWSHOES

Snowshoes are the way to go in the non-motorized regions of the north woods. Even the ruffed grouse gets snowshoes for winter as it grows extra feathers on its feet so it, too, can navigate on the snow-clad ground. This past winter I took Traditions' Crockett Small Game Rifle back to a favorite snowshoe rabbit hunting ground of my youth. Trying to place a .32 lead pea in the shoulders of a rabbit that can jump 10 feet from a standing position and 15 feet on the run is beyond my shooting skills. It was hard enough getting in position for a rifle shot at a sitting snowshoe rabbit.

Tracking this white rabbit, with its five-toed front feet and four-toed hind feet, familiarizes you with the design of the ultimate snowshoe. Long guard hairs over densely haired feet serve a variety of purposes in both design and function including prevention of heat loss, support in deep snow, good grip on ice, and reducing body scent in the tracks by not allowing snow to stick or build up on their feet. Snowshoes of man have evolved from early northern woodland Indian designs such as the Ojibway, constructed of flexible wood frames webbed with twisted bands of basswood or slippery elm inner bark. I have

Snowshoes for muzzleloader hunters have progressed from early Indian designs, to styles including the slender pike and the semi-bear paw, to modern designs that grip and go in snow country.

always been a stickler for tradition when it comes to snowshoes. I have worn the oval semi-bear paw design for hunting brushy cover and the long narrow pike design with its long tail for covering ground in open timber. Unlike the ski, the snowshoe is not made for speed. But designs in recent years with durable metal frames and flexible webbing, featuring a swiveling harness with cleat tracks, allow the winter woods wanderer to cover a wide variety of terrain as well as climb steep inclines with ease. I have now converted, after trekking in the mountains for many years, to a modern snowshoe designed and made by longtime Adirondack maker Havlick Snow Shoe Company.

Hunting the varying hare on snowshoes is a great way to keep your muzzleloading skills tuned and cure cabin fever.

SUCCESS AT LAST

There is a better chance of catching a snowshoe rabbit out on an overcast day, sunning itself in the breaks in the clouds, than on brilliant, clear days when the hares are holding tight. This requires following the rabbit trails and using your snowshoes to stomp every overhang and clump of cover that tracks lead in and out of to get the occupants moving. Adult hares don't make it easy. They will make a straight dash down a trail or leap sideways and take off leaving a new track. Either way, they start making progressively smaller circles that will lead you right back where you started. Unlike cottontails or squirrels, hunting snowshoe rabbits solo is not a high-percentage hunt in game seen or game taken.

It was partly cloudy that February day when I suited up in a WWII snow parka of my father's and my modern snowshoes and headed into the evergreen swamp with the .32 Crockett percussion rifle. As soon as I entered the cover, fresh rabbit tracks in the newly fallen snow indicated a busy night of feeding. It was quite time consuming, following the hare trails and thrashing covers with my snowshoes. I was afraid my opportunity had come and gone when I missed the rabbit early in the hunt. But I truly enjoy following fresh tracks, any tracks. My afternoon was winding down and I wasn't gaining on the rabbit that I had shot low on. As several tracks intermingled I paused to look around.

My eyes followed a lone set of tracks that left the dense surroundings of the swamp. In long strides the prints headed towards a tall blue spruce, 25 yards away. At the outer limits of a low-hanging bough my eyes locked on a snowshoe rabbit sitting in the classic crouched pose, convinced of its security. The varying hare was slightly quartering away from me. It was a shot waiting to happen. It was just that the white lump of rabbit didn't resemble the bulls-eye I plinked at the shooting range. To clear some limbs I knelt down, then cocked the hammer on the Crockett's 25 grains of Pyrodex P and fired. The sound and smell of a small caliber muzzleloader hung in the softwoods. I have to admit I was more than pleased when the 45-gr. patched ball hit its target.

CONCLUSION

Learning to track and shoot rabbits will provide you with greater confidence when you're confronted with a difficult shooting situation in a woodland whitetail setting. Testing the elements, your navigational skills, and your muzzleloader management and shooting skills during winter on snowshoes at 20 degrees or less, can be frustrating at first. But overcoming the elements of Mother Nature and succeeding at a hunting challenge has its rewards–especially when it makes you a better all-around muzzleloader marksman and hunter.

18

Planning That Special Hunt

During the last 25 years I have been fortunate to take my share of hunting trips with a muzzleloader. Compared to some I have taken many trips, while to others my hunting travel has been marginal. My hunting trips have included three to northern Quebec for caribou, two trips to Wyoming for mule deer and pronghorn, three trips to Colorado for elk, a bighorn sheep hunt in the La Garita Mountains in southern Colorado, and a moose hunt in Maine. But the whitetail has remained my number one hunting interest. Besides New York and Pennsylvania, I have hunted whitetail on both sides of the Mississippi in the 1990s from Illinois to Tennessee, including Iowa, Missouri, and Kentucky. The majority have been great trips with great guides and outfitters.

Unfortunately, there also have been a few flops, too, with genuine jackasses parading as outfitters. I have been wadded in a house trailer in Illinois with 18 other unsuspecting clients, and I have been on a "sure thing" caribou hunt where the caribou had left the country long before our arrival. The one thing I have learned: planning your hunting trip starts with YOU!

RESEARCH AND PLANNING

After I had concluded a career as a professional firefighter, my wife suggested I book a special hunting trip–a big elk hunt, say–to commemorate my departure from the fire service. But after thinking about it, I knew I wanted to hunt whitetails. So for my retirement autumn, I planned a bow hunt in Tennessee with friends who live there. I had also booked, two years in advance, a Wyoming whitetail hunt.

Planning the Tennessee trip was a casual affair that required only airline tickets and the shipping of my gear.

Research is the key to locating reputable outfitters and guides who will make your special hunt a success.

The Wyoming trip was the result of research to find the type of quality hunt I wanted for this special occasion. It included outfitter booking, license applications, airline scheduling, shipping guns and gear, and the return of game, guns and gear. Having organized hunting trips for a corporation's clients on a couple of occasions, I had some insight in finding a good outfitting service.

It wasn't until other people were depending on my advice, however, that I really began to research outfitters and find one who could be trusted to provide a quality experience. About three years ago a friend's wife called and asked if I would help her arrange a birthday surprise hunt for her husband. So I proceeded to check out hunts from Alberta to Alabama for whitetails, elk, mule deer and pronghorn antelope.

The best hunt for her money was a pronghorn hunt in Wyoming. Research reacquainted me with an old friend. In 1983 I was the first paid client for Mike Henry's 88 Ranch Outfitting north of Douglas, Wyo. I hunted pronghorn and mule deer again with him in 1985 with my father, brother, and friends. It was great talking with Mike again to hear how his business has grown over the years. I ended up doing an article about his son Garrett who at 14 bagged a huge bull elk (340 Pope & Young) with a bow. Mike also mentioned that whitetails were taking up residence in the river bottoms. Booking only two hunters per year for whitetails has resulted in quality, successful outings. Let's see, two hunters in endless miles of river bottom on a 30,000-acre ranch. Hmmmm…

CHOOSING AN OUTFITTER

Although I had known Mike Henry for 20 years, booking him for a special hunt was not done on acquaintance alone. I still checked references and talked to clients who had been there. Many were repeat clients. During the last decade, Mike has trimmed his hunter numbers down, built a new bunkhouse for hunter's quarters, and practiced quality game management. Pronghorn and mule deer that were exceptional when I hunted there in

Sighting in your rifle after travel removes doubts and instills confidence.

the '80s are the norm today. This past year a client took an exceptional 80-inch pronghorn buck, and several clients took mule deer bucks with 26 to 28 inch spreads. And these are prairie mule deer, not the mountain mule deer known for their antler spread. Mike also books bow hunters. After reading the account of one such bow hunter who had taken a pronghorn and a dandy whitetail buck, I was thoroughly satisfied. After a short call to my friend Don Robbins, we booked the whitetail hunt with Mike Henry, 88 Ranch Outfitters, 1937 Ross Road, Douglas, Wyo., 82633, (307) 358-5941.

Choosing an outfitter is just that. It is your choice. It is your money. Sources for guides and outfitting services include magazine ads, articles on hunts, word of mouth from other hunters, game departments, and outfitter and guide associations in the U.S. and Canada. For example, when searching Wyoming you can contact the Wyoming Outfitter & Guides Association at P.O. Box 2284, Cody, Wyo., 82414, 307-527-7453. The Wyoming Department of Natural Resources (www.dnrlistings.com) will give you the address of each state's DNR for their hunting seasons, game reports and guide associations. When researching Alberta, the Canadian whitetail province with a 40% success rate, I contacted The Professional Outfitters Association of Alberta at P.O. Box 60712 Meadowlark Park Post Office, Edmonton, Alberta T5R 5Y3, 403-486-3050. A little research will get you looking in the right places for the right hunt for you.

Once you contact an outfitter whose hunting interests you, get a list of hunter references. Since you will be spending several thousand dollars, money invested in phone calls to talk to past clients is money well spent. Whitetail hunter success on free-ranging deer in the 40% range is realistic as I have been in the other 60% on numerous whitetail hunts. But don't get hung up on success ratios that are too good to be true. The quality of the hunt, as well as the game hunted, are both important considerations.

Gathering hunter references, although referred because they were successful, will give you a feel for the services provided. Repeat customers are there for a reason. An established outfitter knows his area and the game within it well. Since you are a muzzleloader hunter, does the outfitter have a clue how to work with primitive arms hunters and set up close for game encounters? In the early '80s, I was the first muzzleloader client in camp on several occasions. If the operation doesn't cater to your style of hunting, look elsewhere.

Booking a hunt also includes your own boundaries such as monetary and physical. The cheapest hunt is generally not the best. The outfitter has to make up the money by hosting more hunters, a practice that lowers overall individual success rates. If you can afford top dollar, you still need to do your homework to make sure the outfitter does provide top dollar services. But there are plenty of mid-range, quality outfitters out there to suit your needs.

Your physical ability is also a consideration. Don't book a hunt you aren't capable of. As a client you should be completely prepared for the hunt your outfitter provides: physically prepared for the challenge, geared appropriately for the hunt, and capable of taking game with your muzzleloader. And if you have any physical problems, let the outfitter know beforehand so he can accommodate you. Steve Shoop of J&S Trophy Hunts in Iowa ([660] 945-3736) constructed a ground blind for my 78-year old father after he had knee replacement surgery. Shoop's efforts contributed to an enjoyable and successful hunt for my dad.

LICENSES/TICKETS/SHIPPING

Booking your outfitter should not be a last-minute thing. A year in advance is a minimum buffer. Once you have selected your outfitter, a deposit is usually required. Then it is time to apply for licenses and permits. Whereas my license for the Tennessee bow hunt could be bought over the counter at the time of the hunt, the application period for the Wyoming license was from January 1 to March 31. A quality outfitter will help you through this process by providing the applications and the information to help you fill them out correctly.

Filling out the applications correctly and mailing them in on time are your responsibility. Personal checks are usually not accepted. Make sure you send a cashier's check or a bank or postal money order. You won't be hunting unless you have a license. Take the time and do it correctly and on time.

While many hunters drive to their destination, others do not have the time to travel great distances. Airline tickets must be booked well in advance these days. Airline travel has taken on new dimensions since 9/11/01. I have personally found air travel more orderly and timely since security checks have become the normal way of life in airports. Weather delays are still weather delays. But plan ahead and book your flights. Tickets today come in the form of the traditional printed tickets, or a printed sheet of paper with identification and flights called, and E-ticket (electronic ticket).

I still use a travel agent, but many people purchase their tickets over the internet. The only thing I take to the airport when flying to a hunting trip is a shoulder bag. And think about what you carry in your carry-on bag. I watched a man get upset because security removed his pocketknife. THINK before you pack. The rule of thumb these days is airport arrival 1-½ to 2 hours ahead of departure for check-in.

Flying with firearms requires check-in and registration at the airport. Allow time for it. In 2001, Canada began requiring visitors to fill out a 10-minute form and register their firearms before a customs officer at $50.00 per gun. Times and travel have changed.

Outfitter Steve Shoop with the buck bagged from a ground blind he constructed for the author's father.

HUNT PLANNING CHECK LIST

1) Research Considerations:
    a) Type of hunt offered
    b) Hunter referrals
    c) Accommodations
    d) Transportation to and from airport
    e) Trophy care and meat handling
    f) Assistance in the license application process.
2) Book hunt a minimum of a year in advance/ secure with $ deposit
3) File license applications correctly and on time with cashier's check or money order
4) Make all travel arrangements well in advance
5) Ship gear two weeks prior to hunt (UPS pickup number 800-742-5877)

FLYING WITH FIREARMS

The Transportation Security Administration states, "Firearms carried as checked baggage must be unloaded, packed in a locked hard-sided case, and declared to the airline check-in. Only you, the passenger, may have the key or combination. Ammunition may be packed in the same locked container as the firearm, so long as it is not loaded in the firearm." For more information on TSA firearm regulations contact www.tsa.gov or call (202)366-9900.

Check your airline's rules for firearms handling so you are prepared for check-in when you arrive at the airport. Ironically it was on the 1985 hunt to Mike Henry's when all my hunting gear never made it to Wyoming. Since that time I have used UPS to ship all my gear to the outfitter well in advance of a hunt. Muzzleloaders are legal to ship direct, unlike centerfire rifles. I have the outfitter obtain blackpowder or Pyrodex for my muzzleloader hunts because airlines take a dim view of carrying such regulated materials on passenger flights

I use heavy-duty duffel bags, footlockers, and steel cases for my camera gear, hunting gear and implements. UPS has always got the gear there and back on time. But despite the conscientious care that is no doubt lavished on shipped parcels, shipping containers sometimes get whacked pretty badly en route. I will be getting a steel footlocker to match my steel double gun/bow case. But shipping in advance is hassle-free and gives you peace of mind in the knowledge that your gear is already in the outfitter's possession by the time you arrive.

A HUNT TO REMEMBER

Flash forward: in mid-November, Don Robbins and I headed for our long-awaited hunt in Wyoming at Henry Ranch. Hunting river bottom bucks proved to be different and fun. There are no trees on the high plains of Wyoming. All the cover is in the form of towering cottonwoods bordering dense thickets of Russian olive trees in the riverbeds. And of course you know where the whitetails live: right in the thickets in the bottoms. Instead of acorns, the deer eat the Russian olive with its pit and the fertile prairie grasses of the moist riverbeds. Hunting these whitetails consists of walking the bordering high grounds and glassing the endless miles of tree lined bottoms, attempting to spot whitetails among the thickly-foliated olive trees. The mule deer often boil up onto the plains, but the whitetails stay low and hug the covers. The rut was in full swing, and Don and I would encounter 47 does and 24 bucks before the hunt was over.

On day three of the hunt I was able to succeed in taking a very unique, older buck with 10 points, two small kicker points off of tines, and two amazing 6-inch drop tines. It was a crisp, clear morning when Mike Henry's son Garrett and I glassed him. The buck was working a scrape about an hour after daylight in a river bend about a mile from camp. This whitetail was all I could have hoped for after all the planning and anticipation.

Mike Henry sighed in relief, as he had been watching the buck right up to two weeks before our arrival. Then the buck had disappeared with the onset of the rut. Not that there weren't any deer around, but Mike wanted one of us to take the aging buck. And I couldn't have been happier. To top it off, my friend Don made a great 120-yard muzzleloading shot on a handsome white-racked buck at sunset on the last evening. Mike's sons Garrett and Blake and I had walked off a long stretch of bottom that put the buck right past Don and Mike Henry. As the group gathered for the camera in the last light of the cold day, red-faced hunters smiled for photos, pictures that will forever stir memories of a very special whitetail hunt.

19

The Longhunter Muzzleloading Big Game Record Book

"I got up just as the sun was rising, and a little way down on the shore of the lake I saw a buck. Wal, he was one of 'em - that buck was. The horns on his head were like an old-fashioned rocking chair, and if they hadn't a dozen prongs on 'em, you may skin me."

S. H. Hammond, Wild Northern Scenes, 1857.

TROPHY GAME MORE THAN STATISTICS

Hunters have always admired exceptional animals of a big game species. Reading S.H. Hammond's *Muzzleloading Adventures in the Adirondack Mountains* only fueled my enthusiasm for hunting the same mountains with the same guns 125 years later. Although I had successfully hunted whitetails, what I considered my first trophy game was the first whitetail that I tracked down and shot with a .45 percussion rifle, a large whitetail doe. A dozen years later I found myself in the heart of S.H. Hammond country, in a 20-square-mile wilderness with a partner on a backpacking whitetail hunt. Planning the hunt, putting in the effort of scouting ahead of time, and setting aside a block of time to hunt produced a true trophy moment as I rattled in a huge whitetail buck that possessed a 10-point rack with 26-inch beams that scored 161 and a massive body that still weighed 212 lbs. four days later after being packed out in pieces.

Being a reader of Theodore Roosevelt's hunting books *The Wilderness Hunter, Hunting Trips of A Ranchman,* and *Outdoor Pastimes of an American Hunter,* I knew it was inevitable that I should head to the high plains with a

double-barrel muzzleloader much as Roosevelt did when he first ventured to the region in the early 1880s. In 1983, I had seen a small advertisement for hunting Pronghorns at the 88 Ranch Outfitters in Douglas, Wyo., in the pages of the National Muzzle Loading Rifle Association publication *Muzzle Blasts*. A century after Teddy hunted the high plains I was looking down the barrels of my percussion double rifle at a handsome 15-inch-plus pronghorn buck. I overestimated the range in the wide-open plains and shot right over his back. A day later I did succeed on a heavy-horned buck with, unique forked cutters.

I was so proud of that muzzleloader trophy that it was the first big game animal that I had mounted. Effort, excitement and memory are why that pronghorn hangs on the wall. The fact that it scores 70-2/8 inches of horn and qualifies for the *Longhunter Muzzleloading Big Game Record Book* is the icing on the cake.

A trophy is a different thing to different people. It is a term usually used to describe an outstanding animal, an unusually large specimen. An animal that is large enough to be listed in the *Longhunter Muzzleloading Big Game Record Book* is truly a trophy animal, and no one can argue that point. But even animals that are not large enough to "make the book" but were an outstanding challenge to take are truly trophy animals.

Having been fortunate enough to hunt members of the entire deer family, I was always pleased to take a fine representation of the species. This rarely resulted in a record book head. I remember the time three Colorado bull elk were bugling their heads off, thrashing trees with their antlers within a hundred yards of me. Finally, the biggest bull stepped into the clear and I shot him. I was thoroughly caught up in the moment and proud of this muzzleloading accomplishment.

Muzzleloader hunters didn't have an official journal in which to document trophy game until 1988. Today, in the fourth edition of the *Longhunter Muzzleloading Big Game Records Book*, National Muzzle Loading Rifle Association Executive Director Joyce Vogel has put together another outstanding tribute to muzzleloader hunters and their trophy-class big game animals. The original big game records club is Boone & Crockett, founded in 1887 by Theodore Roosevelt. Boone & Crockett's Fair Chase statement was the first document to outline a code of conduct and ethics for sportsman, and it later became the cornerstone of the game laws we have today.

The *Longhunter Muzzleloading Big Game Record Book* measuring standards are the middle ground between Boone & Crockett's high-end measuring minimums and Pope & Young's lower minimums for the bow hunter. The Longhunter's standard of "fair chase," the ethical rules that hunters observe during the pursuit of game, will not accept candidacy of trophies not acquired under the concept of fair chase. The Longhunter recognizes 32 species and subspecies of North American big game animals for record

book eligibility based on minimum entry scores, defined boundaries, and other factors. To be considered for inclusion in the record book, a trophy must also be accompanied by a score chart completed by an official Longhunter measurer, a field report and hunter information sheet, a notarized Fair Chase statement signed by the hunter, photos of the game head from front and sides, a copy of the hunter's valid hunting license, and a copy of the check-in tag. Not what you'd call skimpy documentation!

When planning a hunt for trophy game, you need to do your homework to find an area that produces the trophy game, find an outfitter that caters to muzzleloader hunters, and book a primetime hunting slot. I followed this recipe in 1998 when booking a whitetail hunt. The first week of the December hunt in Iowa featured balmy 65-degree days and deer that were not to be seen. But fortunately a harsh weather front and a 35-degree drop in temperature got the deer moving. In 24 hours the outfitter experienced his best hunter success ever with 13 hunters bagging 10 bucks. My 10-pointer with a 22-inch spread that qualified for the Longhunter record book was the fifth largest buck taken, with the two biggest scoring over 170. I was in the right place at the right time.

As you review the pages of the Longhunter record book you will see some names that appear more often than others. This is not coincidental. These hunters either live in close proximity to regions known for trophy-class game or put themselves in regions known for trophy-class game. You cannot hunt record class game animals without being where record class animals dwell. The quickest way to find out where the top geographical trophy regions are by species is the Longhunter book.

When you open the book, start by checking where the entries are produced. Regional entries for the five most popular game animals are as follows: for American elk, New Mexico rules the top entries. Utah is tops for the highest-ranking mule deer. Arizona produces the most trophy pronghorns. The larger distribution of the black bear is indicated by the top five entries that range from Saskatchewan, Wisconsin, Alaska, Ontario and Arizona. The expansive range of the whitetail, as one would expect, results in multiple pockets of proven trophy areas. The world-record muzzleloading whitetail that scored a colossal 193-2/8 inches of antler was taken in Saskatchewan in 1992.

Some world records, such as Mike Bowen's 204-4/8 Utah mule deer, are the result of a resident hunter focusing on a secluded area for the trophy buck. Sitka blacktail deer record holder James Baichtall was introduced to the quality bucks on Dall Island, Alaska, through his work as a geologist for U.S. Forest Service. But it still took him several years to get the drop on a 121-6/8 buck with his custom .54 Jim Bridger Hawken. Then there are the patient trophy hunters such as Al Raychard, who passed up several dozen record class Newfoundland bulls before finding what he was looking for, the World Record woodland caribou that scored 323-2/8 inches of antler.

Serious trophy hunters use all of the gun-muzzle-loader-bow record books to track trophy game. An excellent resource for mapping trophy game is the "Geographic Analysis" from the Boone & Crockett Club. These analyses indicate the areas with the best trophy potential, by species, and provide a history of the range. Editor of Boone & Crockett's publication *Fair Chase* is Debra Bradbury. Her late husband Basil has 32 entries in the B&C record book. None were secured by accident. Basil researched, studied maps, and defined areas often for years before embarking on the hunt for trophy game.

Bowhunter Chuck Adams' elk success was the direct result of information derived from the record books. The top elk spots in the Pope & Young Record book are occupied by bulls taken in Coconino County, Ariz. In the *Longhunter Muzzleloading Big Game Record Book*, five of the top 10 bull elk were taken in Catron County, N. M. But Adams' research in the Boone & Crockett book revealed a Wyoming area that had yielded the most 400-inch-plus bulls. His trophy planning produced a 409 2/8 World Record Pope & Young bow elk.

The muzzleloading hunter with the most entries in the Longhunter book is Jim Shockey. His commitment to trophy hunting has allowed him to become the first hunter to complete the Ultimate Slam (all 32 species) of North American game with a muzzleloader.

20

Muzzleloading's Tomorrow Is Today

"With a gun goes responsibility and if a boy is mature enough to own a gun, then he will be responsible with it. . . . With his gun - and a little imagination – he will tread silently in the footprints of the Mountain Men."

The Ted Trueblood Hunting Treasury, *"Of Boys and Guns,"* 1978.

During the summer months a wooden longbow hangs on a hook with a quiver and arrows by my back door. Although my wife and I don't have children, our home has seen a steady flow of nieces and nephews, as well as the kids of friends and visitors. A number of years ago I made an astute observation. Little kids and projectiles are as natural as the daily arc of the sun.

Whether it's badminton birdies, snowballs, rocks, or whiffle balls, their natural instinct is to find a throwable object and fling it at something. Anything! By the time they become eight, nine, or 10, boys and girls become target-selective. The bow and arrow target butts in our backyard suddenly become a curiosity factor. The kids are intrigued with the bow tackle, will stand still for safety and shooting instruction, and smile from ear to ear if their arrows hit anywhere near a target. The reaction of parents in seeing the enjoyment of their children participating in a supervised shooting sport has been amazing. For some of the children, bow shooting at our house was and is a novelty. But for some, it has become the foundation for things to come.

CONCERNED PARENTS

William Peabody is 12 years old and lives with his parents, Debby and Bill, in the pro-gun state of Virginia, in

The hands-on excitement of supervised muzzleloading is a natural for young shooters.

the anti-gun county of Fairfax. William has been visiting our home in the Adirondack foothills annually for at least 10 years. As a roller-hockey goalie he has become known as "Will the Wall." Debby and Bill got William into scouting at an early age. Now a Boy Scout, he likes the monthly camping trips while his parents like the increased responsibility and self-sufficiency they have seen in William. While William was earning his Criminal Prevention Merit Badge, a policeman spoke on gun safety. Through the Boy Scouts of America and the NRA, William has been able to have firearm instruction and shoot a .22 rifle.

As a parent, Bill Peabody feels that firearm instruction not only represents knowledge versus ignorance but that knowledge equals safety. Showing children at an early age what firearms can do, and emphasizing the responsibilities that accompany firearms, takes all the mystery out of them. Kids who handle guns in an adult-regulated environment will not be antisocial, thrill-seeking criminals-to-be. In Bill's own words, "Firearm handling and instruction, of which the best youth instruction is provided by the NRA, diffuses the intrigue. But unfortunately for William, he can't even own a BB gun where we live."

UNEXPECTED INQUIRY

William has become an enthusiast about American history at school and at home. The Revolutionary War is his favorite. William thoroughly enjoys his school class where they recreate battle scenes and debate them. This last year I received a phone call from William. He was in a debate over the effective range of the muzzleloaders used in the Revolutionary War. Not a bad question for a kid whose only exposure to war is the Desert Storm photos of guided missile hits on enemy targets!

It is amazing just how correct you want to be with an uncommon question from a new-millennium kid. I started by telling him that the tide was turned in the Battle of Saratoga by a muzzleloader shooter named Daniel Murphy who made a 300-yard shot with a "rifled" Kentucky rifle on General Fraser at a critical moment in the battle. (Truth be known, it took Murphy three shots to hit General Fraser.)

A NEW SHOOTER

Just prior to the Peabody's visit this last summer I got a call from Bill. Usually during their stay Bill, William, and I slip away for a morning of shooting at the local rifle club or a remote hunting camp with a small range. Bill asked if me William could shoot this year. I said sure, I had a .22 that would be perfect. Bill quickly pointed out that William wanted to shoot a muzzleloader. I responded, "That can be arranged." My father and I just happened to have a nice, classic looking 32-caliber percussion model from Traditions called the Crockett Small Game Rifle. This 49-inch half-stock 6.7 lbs. rifle seemed

Kids love projectiles and respond to supervised shooting sports.

William's parents feel that firearm instruction not only represents knowledge versus ignorance, but that knowledge equals safety.

just the ticket to give William the feel of a traditionally styled muzzleloader with the ballistics and recoil of a .22 long rifle. A little range time before the company arrived had the Crockett shooting a decent target at 25 yards.

William couldn't wait to shoot a muzzleloader. On a clear morning we headed for hunting camp and some shooting. I was relieved to see how well the Crockett fit the lanky young shooter. The hands-on of muzzleloading is a natural for kids. William was fascinated with the components consisting of a 45-gr. ball, a lubricated patch, and a 20-gr. charge of FFFg blackpowder. He was aware of the affects of rifling and grasped the reason for a patched .310" lead ball in a 32-caliber opening. Bill and I covered gun safety and operation.

With shooting-glasses and ear protection in place, William snapped some #11 caps and got a feel for the double set trigger on the rifle. With the Crockett clamped between his knees and the muzzle at a safe angle William commenced loading. First the pre-measured powder charge, then the small ball and patch patch. As he excitedly went for the ramrod, I showed him the ball starter and he quickly introduced the patched ball into the muzzle. I had procured one of Traditions' Durable Range Rods for the loading and cleaning procedures. William was preparing to ram the patched ball home when we headed him off. With guidance, William saw the benefit of a lubricated patch and the load seated in one smooth motion.

Finally, the long-anticipated shot was about to happen. For starters William tried the sitting position. Once he was seated, I handed him the gun. With his shooting hand out of the way I cocked the hammer and set the trigger for him. He put his hand back, lined up the sights and squeezed the trigger. There wasn't any recoil from the tiny charge, just a crisp crack and a cloud of smoke. For the next hour, William's enthusiasm was nonstop. Loading the rifle, shooting sitting and prone, walking to the target and checking the results captivated him. Hitting the bull at 25 yards was a challenge at first, but being a quick and attentive learner, William finished the session with several shots in the black, an accomplishment he and his father were proud of. What better way to end an introduction to muzzleloading than on a positive note?

That day, I witnessed something besides a fine young man having the time of his life. If I'm not mistaken, I witnessed the beginning of a lifelong interest in the shooting sports.

A GROWING EXPERIENCE

Hunting with my father and grandfather was all I knew because I was brought along on hunts starting in 1962 when I was seven. There was no discussion about it; upland game hunting was just a way of life. My mother ruled a male-oriented household with a paint stick kept in the back pocket of her knee length clam diggers. There was no debating a parent in those days. This no-nonsense approach to life must have worked because I now run the family's 50-year-old building business and my parents live less than a mile away. My mother is still the secretary, and my semi-retired father has taken on the nickname R&D (research and development) for his interest in shooting, hunting, and testing many of the muzzleloaders I write about today.

When I received my first .22 caliber rifle I never felt so grown up so suddenly. The responsibility bestowed upon me, and the privilege to hunt with my father and grandfather, along with their guidance, were not taken lightly. Responsible gun handling and shooting were the criteria for choosing the friends I hunted with. It didn't take long to begin to refuse to hunt with anyone I considered careless around our dogs or me. These were decisions that seemed tough at the time but simple in comparison to the decisions of adult life. A 40-acre woodlot back then would keep me and my after-school hunting friends busy for a whole season running rabbits, chasing grouse, and imagining the buck that made a deer track. Those days spent learning responsible gun handling, shooting and hunting helped me develop the alertness, patience, and the skills of observation that I possess today. It was a growing experience that is now becoming all too rare.

Urban sprawl that has consumed over 30 million acres of farmland since 1970 and the accompanying loss of habitat for the target shooter, hunter, and game are what face 12-year olds such as William Peabody and their parents today. As more city-dwelling families drift farther from their rural roots, the shooting and hunting that used to be a part of rural living are no longer activities. They are now an opinion. Dr. John Applegate's study on anti-hunting sentiment concludes, "The greatest opposition to hunting comes from college age females living in urban areas who know nothing about wildlife." We now have "bio-politics" and the "social carrying capacity" based not on facts but on political pressure that will dictate where we can shoot and hunt.

So what can we do to pass along our outdoor sports heritage to the next generation? Join and support the NMLRA, for one thing. Founded in 1933, the NMLRA has done more to promote our nation's rich historical muzzleloading heritage than any other organization through educational and cultural venues including match competition, hunting, gunmaking, safety, and historical re-enactments.

Despite our national loss of game habitat, hunting with muzzleloaders–especially muzzleloader whitetail hunting–has never been more popular. This apparent but welcome contradiction is due in part to Whitetails Unlimited. For more than 20 years this conservation organization has promoted sound deer management, whitetail habitat, safe and ethical hunting, and a solid hunting future for whitetail hunters. *Sports Afield* lists Whitetails Unlimited as the eighth-largest wildlife conservation group in the U. S. A., a fact that says something about success of the organization and its mission, "Working for an American Tradition."

But the fact remains that modern living, life styles, and politics are taking their toll on America's youth. You have to do what you can, where you can, when you can to keep our hunting traditions alive. So when a William Peabody calls you with a question, be generous with your time and, if possible, show him how to shoot. Just maybe you can ignite a spark of interest.

The shooting and hunting sports need the next generation. In this instance, William Peabody showed me that muzzleloading's tomorrow IS today.

Afterword

"There is pleasure in the mere buoyant gliding of the birch-bark canoe, with its curved bow and stern; nothing else that floats possesses such grace, such frail and delicate beauty, as this true craft of the wilderness, which is as much a creature of the wild woods as the deer and bear themselves."

Theodore Roosevelt, The Wilderness Hunter, 1893.

National Muzzle Loading Rifle Association
P. O. Box 67
Friendship, IN 47021
(812) 667-5131
nmlra@nmlra.org

Publishers of *Muzzle Blasts*, the NMLRA's monthly magazine, and the Longhunter Muzzleloading Big Game Record Book.

International Blackpowder Hunting Organization
P.O. Box 1180
Glenrock, WY 82637
(307) 436-9817
www.blackpowderhunting.org

Publisher of the quality quarterly *Blackpowder Hunting* magazine, which covers all aspects of blackpowder hunting.

Dixie Gun Works Blackpowder Annual
Pioneer Press
P.O. Box 684, Gunpowder Lane
Union City, TN 38261
(901) 885-0374
www.dixiegunworks.com

This annual publication covering firearms, hunting, living history, Civil War, historical events and artisans has been a reader's favorite for almost 30 years.

Whitetails Unlimited
P. O. Box 720
Sturgeon Bay, WI 54235
(800) 274-5471
www.whitetailsunlimited.com

Since 1982 WTU has been a non-profit organization working to raise funds in support of education, habitat conservation and the preservation of the hunting tradition for the direct benefit of the whitetail deer and other wildlife. Their informative quarterly is *Whitetails Unlimited Magazine*.

National Rifle Association
11250 Waples Mill Road
Fairfax, VA 22030
(877) 672-1000
www.nra.org

The NRA is the organization and the voice that has supported law-abiding shooters and hunters in America for over 100 years. Their publications, *The American Rifleman* and *The American Hunter*, cover every aspect of shooting and hunting and keep you informed of the antics of the anti-gun movement in America and the NRA's perpetual defense of your Second Amendment Rights.

Austin & Halleck Gun Crafters
2150 South 950 East
Provo, UT 84606-6285
(877) 543-3256
www.austin-halleck.com

Makers of the handsome, traditional .50 Mountain Rifle with browned furniture and figured wood in flint or percussion and their modern 420-series bolt-action muzzleloader with beautifully figured and checkered wood stocks.

American Pioneer Powder
20423 State Road 7, #F6-268
Boca Raton, FL 33498
(888) 756-7693
www.americanpioneerpowder.com

Replica blackpowder in FFg and FFFg granulations available in pre-measured loads or their STICKS compressed charges. No sulfur smell and cleans up with water.

Ballistic Products, Inc.
20015 Seventy-Fifth Ave. North, Box 293
Corcoran, MN 55340
(763) 494-9237
www.ballisticproducts.com

A full line of shotgun shooting supplies including chilled lead shot, nickel and copper plated shot, nontoxic shots including BPI Steel, Bismuth No-Tox and Hevi-Shot, shot-wads, shot cups, over-shot cards, and 209-primers for in-line shotguns and rifles.

Barnes Bullets, Inc.
750 North 2600 West
American Fork, UT 84003
(800) 574-9200
www.barnesbullets.com

Creator of the Expander and Spit-Fire MZ all-copper bullets for .45, .50, and .54 muzzleloaders and the Barnes Ballistics program that provides loads, ballistics and trajectory data for the muzzleloading shooter and hunter.

Bass Pro Shops / Redhead
2500 E. Kearney
Springfield, MO 65898
(800) 227-7776
www.basspro.com

A complete line of traditional and modern muzzleloading guns and accessories.

Blackpowder Products, Inc.
5988 Peachtree Corners East
Norcross, GA 30071
(770) 449-4687
www.cva.com & www.powerbeltbullets.com & www.winchestermuzzleloading.com

Home of CVA muzzleloader, Winchester Muzzleloading, and the very popular PowerBelt Bullet.

Blomquist Percussion Works, Ltd
2025 E. 110 St.
Indianapolis, IN 46280
(800) 337-1243
www.bpwltd.net
Custom manufacturer of problem solving percussion nipples and wrenches for in-lines, side locks and under hammers.

BSA Optics
3911 SW Forty-Seventh Ave., Suite 914
Ft. Lauderdale, FL 33314
(954) 581-2144
bsaoptic@bellsouth.net
A full line of sporting optics including scopes, binoculars, spotting scopes, mounts and accessories.

Buffalo Bullet Company, Inc.
12637 Los Nietos Road, Suite A
Santa Fe Springs, CA 90670
(562) 944-0322
Extensive line of lead projectiles including round balls, hollow point/hollow base slugs and the Buffalo Ballet, as well as the SSB, Special Sabot Bullet with a spitzer profile for longer range shooting.

Bushnell Performance Optics
9200 Cody
Overland Park, KS 66214
(800) 423-3537
www.bushnell.com
For over 50 years Bushnell has provided a complete line of quality hunting optics.

CCI/Speer
P.O. Box 856
Lewiston, ID 83501
(800) 627-3640
www.cci-ammunition.com & www.speer-bullets.com
CCI produces #11 percussion caps, musket caps and 209 primers for muzzleloading firearms. Speer produces excellent swaged round balls, as well as jacketed pistol bullets for the sabot shooter.

Cabela's Shooting Catalog
One Cabela's Drive
Sidney, NE 69160
(800) 237-4444
www.cabelas.com
A full section of their catalog is dedicated to muzzleloader hunting firearms and accessories.

Circle Fly Shotgun Wads
4314 Dale Williamson Road
Union, KY 41091
(859) 689-5100
Shotgun wads and over-shot cards for the muzzleloading shotgunner.

D&D Bullets
P.O. Box 1363
Okmulgee, OK 74447
(918) 652-0427
DandDBullets@yahoo.net
Maker of the CSP Deer Bullet.

Dixie Gun Works, Inc.
Gunpowder Lane, P.O. Box 130
Union City, TN 38281
(800) 238-8765
www.dixiegunworks.com
The largest blackpowder catalog; conveniently indexed to guide you through 736 pages and 10,000 items relating to blackpowder guns, shooting supplies and antique gun parts.

Dynamit-Nobel-RWS
81 Ruckman Rd.
Closter, NJ 07624
(201) 767-1995
www.dnrws.com
A variety of percussion caps for the muzzleloading rifle and shotgun shooter.

Express Sight Systems
2401 Ludelle St.
Fort Worth, TX 76105
(888) 774-4880
www.expresssights.com
Makers of the A.O. Express Ghost Ring Hunting Sights and the Ashley Power Rod.

Gerber
P.O. Box 23088
Portland, OR 97224
(503) 639-6161
www.gerberblades.com
Legendary hunting knives as well as field tools such as the Deluxe Hunter's Pruning Kit.

Goex, Inc.
P.O. Box 659
Doyline, LA 71023
(318) 382-9300
www.goexpowder.com
The oldest manufacturer of blackpowder in the United States; founded 1812.

Hodgdon Powder Company
6321 Robinson Rd., P.O. Box 2932
Shawnee Mission, KS 66201
(913) 362-9455
www.hodgdon.com
Makers of the most popular replica blackpowder Pyrodex in P, RS, and Select granulations; the Pyrodex Pellet; and the new Triple Seven in FFg and FFFg granulation and in Pellet form.

Hornady Manufacturing Company
P.O. Box 1848
Grand Island, NE 68803
(308) 382-1390
www.hornady.com
Noted for the Great Plains Maxi-Bullet, swaged round balls and the XTP Mag sabot bullets.

Hunter Specialties, Inc.
6000 Huntington CT NE
Cedar Rapids, IA 52402
(319) 395-0321
www.hunterspec.com
Distributors of the True Talker Deer Call and the country's largest manufacturer of hunting calls and hunting accessories.

Knight Rifles
21852 Highway J46, P.O. Box 130
Centerville, IA 52544
(641) 856-2626
www.knightrifles.com
Tony Knight put the modern muzzleloader on the map in 1985 with the MK-85, the bolt-action Disc Rifle in the 1990s, and now the latest Knight design, the pivoting block trigger assembly and the Revolution Rifle.

Knight & Hale Game Calls
3601 Jenny Lind Rd.
Fort Smith, AR 72901
(501) 782-8971
www.knight-hale.com
Manufacturer of deer, turkey, predator, squirrel and waterfowl calls andd instructional videos.

Leupold & Stevens Inc.
P.O. Box 688
Beaverton, OR 97075
(503) 526-1421
www.leupold.com
Manufacturers of a complete line of scopes, binoculars, spotting scopes and mounting systems. All Leupold "Golden Ring" products are made in the USA.

Lyman Products Corp.
475 Smith Street
Middletown, CT 06457
(800) 225-9626
www.lymanproducts.com
Lyman offers a complete line of gun sights, bullet-casting tools for muzzleloaders, great shooting rifles including their Great Plains Hunter Rifle, and The Lyman Black Powder Handbook & Loading Manual by Sam Fadala.

Magellan Systems Corp.
960 Overland Court
San Dimas, CA 91773
(909) 394-5000
www.thalesnavigation.com
Complete line of Magellan GPS navigational units.

Michaels Of Oregon
P.O. Box 1690
Oregon City, OR 97045
(503) 655-7964
www.michaels-oregon.com
Uncle Mike's slings, shooting bags and hunting accessories have long been a standard in the muzzleloading industry.

Mountain State Muzzleloading Supplies
MSM, Inc.
P.O. Box 324
Williamstown, WV 26187
(304) 295-6959
www.msmfg.com
Manufacturers of the Super-Rod, the "original" replacement rod for muzzleloaders, as well as a complete line of muzzleloader shooting accessories.

Muzzleload Magnum Products
518 Buck Hollow Lane
Harrison, AR 72601
(870) 741-5019
www.mmpsabots.com
MMP is the company that put the sabot on the map. Their new MMP Ballistic Bridge Sub-Base, when seated over the powder charge, beneath the sabot bullet, is the answer for achieving top performance and reclaiming the accuracy of hot hunting charges.

Navy Arms Co.
219 Lawn Street
Martinsburg, WV 25401
(304) 262-9870
www.navyarms.com
Distributor of historically correct firearms including their new Lewis and Clark 1803 Harpers Ferry Rifle.

October Country Muzzleloading, Inc.
P.O. Box 969
Hayden, ID 83835
(800) 735-6348
www.octobercountry.com
Keeping traditional shooters outfitted with the finest shooting bags, powder horns, and accessories since 1977.

Ox-Yoke Originals
34 W. Main St.
Milo, ME 04463
(207) 943-7351
www.oxyoke.com
The makers of Wonder Lube, Wonder Wads, superior cleaning and loading rods, cleaning kits, and a full line of accessories for loading, shooting, and cleaning muzzleloaders.

Pete Rickard's Inc.
Cobleskill, NY 12043
(518) 234-2731
www.peterickard.com
Pete Rickard didn't realize he was creating an industry when he developed Original Indian Buck Lure in 1934. A full line of deer hunting, trapping, cover scents, training scents and odor eliminators, as well as deer, turkey, predator, and waterfowl calls.

R.E. Davis Company
P.O. Box 752
Perrysburg, OH 43552
(419) 833-1200
www.redaviscompany.com
One of the leaders in manufacturing muzzleloading firearm components that include the Davis Deerslayer replacement triggers.

Remington Arms Co., Inc.
P.O. Box 700
Madison, NC 27025
(800) 243-9700
www.remington.com
The muzzleloading Model 700 ML patterned after the popular 700 series is a real favorite for Remington shooters. Also percussion caps and accessories.

Savage Arms
118 Mountain Road
Suffield, CT 06078
www.savagearms.com
Creators of the Savage 10ML-II, the "smokeless powder" muzzleloader, that also shoots blackpowder and blackpowder substitutes.

Schuetzen Powder, LLC.
7650 US Hwy. 287, 100
Arlington, TX 76001
(866) 809-9704
www.schuetzenpowder.com
Distributors of quality Schuetzen Black Powder, Swiss Black Powder, and Elephant Black Powder.

Segway Industries
P.O. Box 783
Suffern, NY 10901
(845) 357-5510
http://www.segway-industries.com/
Maker of the handy to use scope Reticle Leveler.

Simmons Outdoor Corporation
201 Plantation Oak Drive
Thomasville, GA 31792
(800) 285-0689
www.simmonsoptics.com
For 20-years Simmons have provided quality riflescopes, binoculars, spotting scopes and accessories including their excellent Bore Sighter Kit.

Stoney Point Products, Inc.
1822 North Minnesota St.
New Ulm, MN 56073
(507) 354-3360
www.stoneypoint.com
Shooting sticks and rests such as the Hike 'N Hunt staff/bipod combo.

TDC
201 South Klein Drive
P.O. Box 130
Waunakee, WI 53597
(608) 849-5664
www.tdcmfg.com
Tedd Cash's new Straight Line 209 primer dispenser is the latest addition to the finest line of priming accessories on the market today.

Tru-Glo Inc.
13745 Neutron Rd.
Dallas, TX 75244
P. O. Box 1612
McKinney, TX 75070
(972) 744-0300
www.truglosights.com
Complete line of fiber optic aiming devices.

Thompson/Center Arms
P.O. Box 5002, Farmington Rd.
Rochester, NH 03867
(603) 332-2333
www.tcarms.com
The company that started it all with the hunting Hawken Rifle just raised the bar again with the introduction of their Encore break-action and the Omega drop-action guns.

Tennessee Valley Muzzleloading Inc.
14 CR 521
Corinth, MS 38834
(662) 287-6021
www.tvm.com
Historically authentic hand crafted muzzleloading rifles and supplies.

Traditions Performance Muzzleloading
1375 Boston Post Rd.
POB 776
Old Saybrook, CT 06475
(860) 388-4656
www.traditionsmuzzle.com
A full line of muzzleloaders and accessories ranging from traditional guns considered "Authentic for Re-enactment" use to the Lightning Bolt-Action Rifle.

Williams Gun Sight Co., Inc.
G-7389 Lapeer Rd.
Davison, MI 48423
(800) 530-9028
www.williamsgunsight.com
Fire Sights fiber optic light-gathering sights for muzzleloaders as well a full line of barrel-mounted sights.

Wildlife Research Center
1050 McKinley Street
Anoka, MN 55303
(800) 873-5873
www.wildlife.com
WRC scents and human scent elimination.

Triple Seven Data

.45 CALIBER

BULLET/SABOT	POWDER MEASURE SETTING Triple Seven FFG				POWDER MEASURE SETTING Triple Seven FFFG			
	70gr.	80gr.	90gr.	100gr.	70gr.	80gr.	90gr.	100gr.
150gr. Knight/Red Hot	1963	2134	2187	2284	2041	2141	2206	2295
180gr. T/C XTP	1916	1993	2054	2108	1936	2003	2103	2225
240gr. Knight Lead PT	1725	1792	1849	1991	1780	1843	1912	2006
225gr. CVA Power Belt	1684	1720	1784	1905	1687	1742	1799	1925

.50 CALIBER

BULLET/SABOT	POWDER MEASURE SETTING Triple Seven FFG				POWDER MEASURE SETTING Triple Seven FFFG			
	70gr.	80gr.	90gr.	100gr.	70gr.	80gr.	90gr.	100gr.
240gr. Hdy. XTP 50/44	1578	1662	1748	1820	1566	1662	1797	N/A
300gr. Nosler Shots 50/44	1466	1606	1645	1713	1462	1609	1651	1729
250gr. Bar. MZ 50/45	1609	1705	1775	1847	1594	1752	1823	1971
260gr. Spr./Blk. Sabot 50/45	1602	1688	1757	1811	1589	1683	1794	1865
300gr. T/C XTP 50/45	1471	1600	1659	1746	1482	1610	1671	1749
348gr. CVA Power Belt	1424	1465	1542	1664	1471	1500	1595	1663
385gr. Hdy. Conical/W/Wad	1329	1423	1517	1613	1360	1461	1541	1605
410gr. Hdy. Conical/W/Wad	1276	1366	1460	1508	1383	1445	1503	1594

.54 CALIBER

BULLET/SABOT	POWDER MEASURE SETTING Triple Seven FFG			
	80gr.	90gr.	100gr.	120gr.
250gr. Nosler Shots 54/45	1523	1625	1789	1884
300gr. T/C Mag. Express 54/45	1578	1632	1741	1841
352gr. Spr./Blk.Sabot 54/50	1531	1622	1692	1775
348gr. CVA Power Belt	1473	1564	1623	1728
360gr. T/C Max Hunter/W/Wad	1439	1524	1604	1691
425gr. Hdy. Great Plains Conical	1354	1423	1499	1587

CAP AND BALL REVOLVER

POWDER MEASURE SETTING Triple Seven FFFG	15gr.	20gr.
36 cal. 1851 Navy Steel Frame		
375 Hdy. RB Ox-Yoke W/Wad	662	832
44 cal. 1858 Rem. Steel Frame	20gr.	25gr.
454 Hdy. RB Ox-Yoke W/Wad	536	763
44 cal. 1860 Army Steel Frame	20gr.	25gr.
451 Spr. RB Ox-Yoke W/Wad	524	592
45 cal. Ruger Old Army	30gr.	35gr.
457 Hdy. RB Ox-Yoke W/Wad	845	987

PATCHED ROUND BALL

PATCHED ROUND BALL	POWDER MEASURE SETTING Triple Seven FFG							
	40gr.	50gr.	60gr.	70gr.	80gr.	90gr.	100gr.	120gr.
45 Caliber								
440 Hdy. RB/.020 Ox-Yoke patch	1534	1692	1926	—	—	—	—	—
50 Caliber								
490 Spr. RB/.020 Ox-Yoke patch	—	—	—	1744	1842	1925	1988	
54 Caliber								
530 Hdy. RB/.020 Ox-Yoke patch	—	—	—	—	1667	1775	1846	1943

PATCHED ROUND BALL	POWDER MEASURE SETTING Triple Seven FFFG							
	40gr.	50gr.	60gr.	70gr.	80gr.	90gr.	100gr.	120gr.
50 Caliber								
490 Spr. RB/.020 Ox-Yoke patch	—	—	—	1801	1873	1945	1997	—

PISTOL AND RIFLE CARTRIDGE

CARTRIDGE	BULLET	POWDER	POWDER MEASURE SETTINGS	VEL. [FPS]	PRESSURE
38 Special	125gr. LRNFP	Triple Seven FFG	20.0gr	931	8,800 CUP
38 Special	158gr. LSWC	Triple Seven FFG	15.0gr	785	7,600 CUP
38-40 WCF	180gr. Cast LRNFP	Triple Seven FFG	30.0gr	887	7,700 CUP
44 SPL	200gr. Cast LRNFP	Triple Seven FFG	25.0gr	907	7,600 CUP
44 SPL	240gr. Cast LSWC	Triple Seven FFG	20.0gr	778	7,400 CUP
44-40 WCF	200gr. Cast LRNFP	Triple Seven FFG	30.0gr	830	6,500 CUP
44 Rem. Mag.	200gr. Cast LRNFP	Triple Seven FFG	30.0gr	984	8,800 CUP
44 Rem. Mag.	240gr. Cast LSWC	Triple Seven FFG	25.0gr	868	9,100 CUP
45 Colt	200gr. Cast LRNFP	Triple Seven FFG	35.0gr	959	8,500 CUP
45 Colt	250gr. Cast LRNFP	Triple Seven FFG	30.0gr	838	9,500 CUP
38-55	250gr. Lyman Cast	Triple Seven FFG	35.0gr	1261	—
40-65 Win.	400gr. Buffalo Arms Lead RNFP	Triple Seven FFG	50.0gr	1152	—
45-70 Govt.	405gr. Cast LFP	Triple Seven FFG	60.0gr	1260	—
45-70 Govt.	485gr. Cast LFP	Triple Seven FFG	60.0gr	1161	—
45-120 Sharps	405gr. Lyman #457193	Triple Seven FFG	95.0gr	1511	—
45-120 Sharps	500gr. Lyman #457125	Triple Seven FFG	95.0gr	1375	—

SHOTGUN

CARTRIDGE	SHOT CHARGE	BARREL LENGTH	CASE	PRIMER	POWDER	POWDER MEASURE SETTINGS	VEL. [FPS]	PRESSURE
12 Gauge, 2 3/4"	1 1/8 oz. Shot	30"	Win. AA Win. AA12R Wad	Win. 209	Triple Seven FFG	70.0gr	1187	7,700 CUP

*WARNING – DO NOT USE **Triple Seven** in shotguns with damascus barrels.

State-by-State Answers To The Most-Asked

	AL	AK	AZ	AR	CA	CO	CT	DE	FL	GA	HI	ID	IL	IN	IA	KS	KY	LA	ME	MD	MA	MI
Are smokeless powders (nitrocellulose-based) legal?	No	Yes*	Yes	Yes	--	Yes	Yes	No	No	Yes	Yes	No	No	Yes	Yes	Yes	Yes	No	--	Yes	No	No
Is there a special muzzleloader season? If so, what are the dates?	Yes*	Yes	Yes*	Yes*	--	Yes*	Yes*	Yes*	Yes*	Yes*	Yes*	Yes*	Yes*	Yes*	Yes*	Yes*	Yes*	Yes*	--	Yes*	Yes*	Yes*
Is a rifled barrel legal for big game?	Yes	Yes	Yes	Yes	Yes	Yes	Yes	Yes	Yes	Yes	Yes	Yes	Yes	Yes	Yes	Yes	Yes	Yes	Yes	Yes	Yes	Yes
Is a smoothbore barrel legal for big game?	Yes	Yes	Yes	Yes	Yes	Yes	No	Yes	Yes	Yes	Yes	Yes	Yes	Yes	Yes	Yes	Yes	Yes	Yes	Yes	Yes*	Yes
What is the minimum caliber for rifled barrels?	.40	*	None	.40	.40	.40*	.45	.42	.40	.44	.44	.45*	.45	.44	.44	.39	None	.44	.40	.40	.44	None
What is the minimum caliber (gauge) for smoothbores?	None	*	None	None	--	.40*	.45	20 ga.	20 ga.	20 ga.	.44	.45*	.45	.44	.44	.39	None	10 ga.	.40	.40	None	None
What is the maximum caliber for rifled barrels?	None	None	None	None	--	None	None	None	None	None	None	None	None	None	.775	None	None	None	None	None	.775	None
What is the maximum caliber (gauge) for smoothbores?	10 ga.	10 ga.	None	None	--	None	None	None	10 ga.	None	None	None	None	None	.775	None	10 ga.	10 ga.	None	None	10 ga.	None
What is the minimum barrel length for smoothbores? For rifled barrels?	18"/18"	None	None	*	--	None	None	None	18"/16"	18"/18"	--	None	16"/16"	None	18-1/2"	None	None	None	--	None	18"/18"	None
What number of barrels are legal?	Any	Any	1	*	--	Any	*	1	1	Any	1	2	2	1*	Any	Any	Any	2	--	Any	1*	Any
Is an in-line ignition legal?	Yes	Yes	Yes	Yes	Yes	Yes	Yes	Yes	Yes	Yes	Yes	No	Yes	Yes	Yes	Yes	Yes*	Yes	Yes	Yes	Yes	Yes
Is a closed breech legal?	Yes	Yes	Yes	Yes	Yes	Yes	Yes	Yes	Yes	Yes	Yes	Yes	Yes	Yes	Yes	Yes	Yes*	Yes	Yes	Yes	Yes	Yes
Are telescopic sights legal?	No	No	Yes	Yes	No	No	Yes	Yes	Yes	Yes	No	Yes	No	Yes	Yes	Yes	No	Yes*	Yes	Yes	Yes	Yes
Are laser sights legal?	No	No	No	Yes	--	No	Yes	Yes	Yes	No	Yes	No	Yes	Yes	No	No	Yes	No	--	Yes	No	No
Are fiber optic sights legal?	Yes	Yes	Yes	Yes	--	Yes	Yes	Yes	Yes	Yes	No	Yes	Yes	Yes	Yes	Yes	Yes	Yes	--	Yes	*	Yes
Is a round ball projectile legal?	Yes	Yes	Yes	Yes	--	Yes	Yes	Yes	Yes	Yes	Yes	Yes	Yes	Yes	Yes	Yes	Yes	Yes	--	Yes	Yes	Yes
Is a conical bullet legal?	Yes	Yes	Yes	Yes*	Yes	Yes	Yes*	Yes	Yes	Yes	Yes	Yes	Yes	Yes/.44	Yes	Yes	Yes	Yes	--	Yes	Yes	Yes
Are sabots legal?	Yes	Yes	Yes	Yes	No	No	Yes	Yes	Yes	Yes	Yes	Yes	Yes	Yes	Yes	Yes	Yes	Yes	--	Yes	Yes	Yes
Are jacketed bullets legal?	Yes	Yes	Yes	Yes*	--	--	Yes	No	Yes*	Yes	Yes	No	Yes*	Yes	Yes	Yes	Yes	Yes	--	Yes	No	Yes
Is there a minimum projectile diameter and/or weight?	No	*	No	*	--	*	.45	.42*	.40	None	None	.428	.44	.44	None	None	None	None	--	None	None	None
Is pelletized powder legal?	Yes	Yes	Yes	Yes	Yes	No	Yes	Yes	Yes	Yes	Yes	Yes*	Yes	Yes	Yes	Yes	Yes	Yes	Yes	Yes	*	Yes
Are 209 primers legal?	Yes	Yes	Yes	Yes	Yes	Yes	Yes	Yes	Yes	Yes	Yes	No	Yes	Yes	Yes	Yes	Yes	Yes	No	Yes	Yes	Yes
Are muzzleloading handguns legal? Any restrictions?	Yes	No	Yes	Yes*	No	No	*	No*	Yes	Yes*	Yes*	No	No	Yes*	Yes*	Yes*	Yes	Yes*	Yes*	Yes	No	Yes

Note: This information was current as of 2003. Hunting regulations change frequently, so always check your state regulations well in advance of hunting season.

Questions About Muzzleloader Hunting

MN	MS	MO	MT	NE	NV	NH	NJ	NM	NY	NC	ND	OH	OK	OR	PA	RI	SC	SD	TN	TX	UT	VT	VA	WA	WV	WI	WY
Yes	No	Yes	No	Yes	--	Yes	No	No	Yes	Yes	Yes	Yes	Yes	No	Yes*	Yes	No	No	Yes	Yes	No	No	No	No	No	--	No
Yes*	Yes*	Yes*	No	Yes*	--	Yes*	Yes*	Yes*	Yes*	Yes*	Yes*	--	Yes*	Yes*	Yes*	Yes*	Yes*	Yes*	Yes*	Yes*	Yes*	Yes*	Yes*	--	Yes*	--	Yes*
Yes	Yes	Yes	Yes	Yes	Yes	Yes	Yes	Yes	Yes	Yes	Yes	Yes	Yes	Yes	Yes	Yes	Yes	Yes	Yes	Yes	Yes	Yes	Yes	Yes	Yes	Yes	Yes
Yes	Yes	Yes	Yes	Yes	Yes	Yes	Yes	Yes	Yes	No	Yes	Yes	Yes	Yes	Yes	Yes	Yes	Yes	Yes	Yes	Yes	Yes	Yes	Yes	Yes	Yes	No
.40	.38	.40	.45	.44	.45	.40/.50*	.44	.45	.44	None	.45	.38	.40	.40/.50*	.44	.45	.36	.44*	.40	None	.40	.43	.45	.40	.38	.40	.40
.45	None	.40	.45	.62	.45	.40	20 ga.	.45	.44	N/A	.45	.410	20 ga.	.40/.50*	.44	20 ga.	20 ga.	.44*	.40/20 ga.	None	None	.43	.45	.60	.38	.45	N/A
None	None	None	None	None	None	None	None	None	None	None	None	None	None	None	None	None	None	None	None	None	None	None	None	None	None	--	None
None	None	10 ga.	None	None	None	None	10 ga.	None	None	N/A	None	10 ga.	None	None	None	None	None	None	None	None	10 ga.	None	10 ga.	None	None	--	N/A
None	18"/16"	18"	Any	Any	None	None	18"/16"	None	16"	16"	None	--	None	18"	18"	18"	None	None	None	None	18"	20"	None	20"	None	--	None
Any	2	Any	2	Any	1	1	1	Any	1	Any	1	--	2	1	1	2	Any	Any	*	Any	1	1	Any*	--	1	--	Any
Yes	Yes	Yes	Yes	Yes	Yes	Yes	Yes	Yes	Yes	Yes	Yes	Yes	Yes	Yes	Yes*	Yes	Yes	Yes	Yes	Yes	Yes	Yes	Yes	Yes	Yes	Yes	Yes
Yes	Yes	Yes	Yes	Yes/1X	No	Yes	Yes	Yes	Yes	Yes	Yes	Yes	Yes	No	Yes*	No	Yes	Yes	Yes	Yes	Yes	Yes	Yes	No	No	No	Yes
No	Yes	Yes	Yes	No	No	Yes	Yes	Yes	Yes	No	No	Yes	Yes	No	Yes*	Yes	Yes	Yes*	Yes	No	Yes	Yes	No	Yes	No	No	Yes
No	Yes	No	No	Yes	--	Yes*	No	--	No	No	No	Yes	No	No	No	Yes	Yes	No	Yes	No	No	Yes	No	No	No	--	No
Yes	Yes	Yes	Yes	Yes	--	Yes	Yes	--	Yes	Yes	Yes	Yes	No	Yes	Yes	No	Yes	Yes	Yes	Yes	Yes	Yes	Yes	No	--	No	No
Yes	Yes	Yes	Yes	Yes	--	Yes	Yes	Yes	Yes	Yes	Yes	Yes	Yes	Yes	Yes	No	Yes	Yes	Yes	Yes	Yes	Yes	--	Yes	--	Yes	Yes
Yes	Yes	Yes	Yes	Yes	Yes	Yes	Yes	--	Yes	Yes	Yes	Yes	Yes*	Yes	Yes	Yes	Yes	Yes	Yes	Yes	Yes	Yes	Yes	Yes	Yes	Yes	Yes
Yes	Yes	Yes	No	Yes	Yes	Yes	Yes	Yes	Yes	Yes	Yes	Yes	Yes	No	Yes	Yes	Yes	Yes	Yes	Yes	Yes	Yes	Yes	Yes	Yes	Yes	Yes
Yes	Yes	Yes*	No	Yes	Yes	Yes	Yes	Yes*	Yes	Yes	Yes	Yes	No	Yes	Yes	Yes	No	Yes	Yes	Yes	Yes	No	Yes	No	Yes	No	Yes
None	None	--	.45	No	--	*	None	--	None	None	.45	--	None	*	None	.43	No	.44	None	No	170/210*	None	.38	--	None	--	No
Yes	Yes	Yes	Yes	Yes	Yes	Yes	Yes	--	Yes	Yes	Yes	Yes	No	Yes	Yes	Yes	Yes	Yes	Yes	Yes	Yes	Yes	No	Yes	Yes	No	Yes
Yes	Yes	Yes	Yes	Yes	No	Yes	Yes	--	Yes	Yes	Yes	Yes	No	Yes*	Yes	Yes	Yes	Yes	Yes	Yes	Yes	Yes	No	Yes	Yes	No	Yes
Yes*	No	Yes	Yes	No	No	Yes	No	--	Yes*	No	Yes*	No	Yes	No	No	No	No	No*	Yes	Yes*	No	Yes*	No	No	Yes*	No	Yes*

Note: This information was current as of 2003. Hunting regulations change frequently, so always check your state regulations well in advance of hunting season.

GOEX MUZZLELOADING LOAD CHART

Note: These are general guidelines only. Some manufacturers will not recommend even these low starting loads in their rifles. **DO NOT EXCEED YOUR RIFLE'S RECOMMENDED MAXIMUM STARTING LOADS AS STATED BY THE MANUFACTURER!** All charges measured by volume, not weight.

CALIBER	ROUNDBALL	CONICAL	SABOT	CHARGE	COMMENTS / RATE OF TWIST
.32 cal	47 gr.			25 gr. 3F	1:48 or slower
.32 cal		60-80 gr.		25 gr. 3F	1:48 or slower
.32 cal		80-105 gr.		30 gr. 3F	1:48
.36 cal	65 gr.			35 gr. 3F	1:48 or slower
.36 cal		80-120 gr.		30 gr. 3F	1:48 or slower
.36 cal		120-130 gr.		35 gr. 3F	1:48 or slower
.36 cal			70-100 gr.	30 gr. 3F	1:48 or faster twist
.40 cal (slow twist)	93 gr.			40 gr. 3F	1:48 or slower
.40 cal (fast twist)	93 gr.			35 gr. 3F	White, Inc. rifles only
.40 cal (fast twist)		275-320 gr.		70 gr. 2F	Note: 2F loads for White, Inc. rifles only
.40 cal (fast twist)		320-400 gr.		70 gr. 2F	Heavier weight, reduce charge; White, Inc. rifles only
.45 cal	127 gr.			70 gr. 2F	For slow twist rifles
.45 cal	127 gr.			60 gr. 2F	For fast twist rifles
.45 cal		200-300 gr.		80 gr. 2F	Use only where allowed by manufacturer
.45 cal		300-400 gr.		85 gr. 2F	Fast twist only
.45 cal			158 gr. in sabot	80 gr. 2F	Fast twist only
.45 cal			200-350 gr. in sabot	80 gr. 2F	Fast twist only
.50 cal	180 gr.			80 gr. 2F	Slow twist
.50 cal	180 gr.			60 gr. 2F	Reduce RB charge in fast twist rifles
.50 cal		245-350 gr.		80 gr. 2F	Medium twist
.50 cal		350-425 gr.		85 gr. 2F	1:48 or faster
.50 cal		425-600 gr.		90 gr. 2F	Use only where allowed by manufacturer
.50 cal			240-300 gr. in sabot	80 gr. 2F	Fast twist rifles only
.50 cal			300-450 gr. in sabot	85 gr. 2F	Fast twist rifles only
.54 cal	220-230 gr.			80 gr. 2F	Slow twist
.54 cal	220-230 gr.			70 gr. 2F	Reduce RB charge in fast twist rifles
.54 cal		350-450 gr.		90 gr. 2F	Medium twist
.54 cal		450-600 gr.		95 gr. 2F	Medium twist
.54 cal			240-300 gr. in sabot	90 gr. 2F	Fast twist only
.54 cal			300-450 gr. in sabot	95 gr. 2F	Fast twist only
.58 cal	280-290 gr.			70 gr. 2F	Slow twist replica firearms
.58 cal	280-290 gr.			75 gr. 2F	Reduce charge for modern, fast twist rifles
.58 cal		450-550 gr.		90 gr. 2F	Modern, rifles 1:48 or faster twist
.58 cal			240-350 gr. in sabot	95 gr. 2F	Fast twist only
.69 & .75 cal	490-525 gr.			70 gr. 2F	Maximum charge for replica rifles